C0-GHB-191

The Home for Friendless Children

C. L. Olsen
Home for Friendless Children
Copyright 2021, C.L. Olsen
All Rights Reserved.

In writing this book, the author has changed the names of some, but not all, individuals and places to preserve anonymity; and Rob did the very best he could to recall his memory of events as accurately as possible.

THE HOME FOR FRIENDLESS CHILDREN

A Memoir

C. L. Olsen

CONTENTS

For

Bob MacGuffie, PhD;

Bonita Cales, LPC; and

Chad Saperstein, PhD;

Thank you.

"To have faith is to have wings."

—Peter Pan

CHAPTER 1

It was harder this time. Because of the cold. And because we were one sheet short. And because it was snowing.

And I had no socks. My mother had cut the foot part off of my pajamas because they got too short. Or because I got too tall. And there was no time to look for shoes.

Tom climbed down first, then jumped the other six feet or so. It looked too far down to me, and I didn't think the worn sheet we had tied to the window crank would hold. But Tom threatened to leave me, so I shimmied down, closed my eyes, and jumped.

The bar below our apartment was dark, the snowy street deserted. We ran.

It was only after we had squeezed through the narrow basement window of the old mill and felt around for the old rugs we had left there in the blackness that my heart eventually stopped trying to bust through my chest. We huddled close in the corner on the broken cement floor—Tom wrapping his rug around my frozen feet, snuggling close together under mine. It was then that I felt the warm blood from the cut on my neck where my pajama collar had dug into my skin as Tom pulled me by the chest as we ran.

Our breath was still hard and fast, and it was so dark. As we watched the first tiny sliver of dawn through the filthy window, we had one thought. One thought only. *Jack.*

CHAPTER 2

I used to count the freckles on her impossibly perfect face. She never looked my way—why would she? But that's OK; it was less painful that way. She would never be mine.

Someone said she had always lived here. Had a job here too. *Responsibilities.* She was that kind of girl. Which meant that I saw her often, as she would come to the younger boy's dormitory every three days to deliver our clean laundry.

She was light of foot, seeming to float instead of walk down the long, dark corridors—carrying this and that, in perfect posture, her soft, brown braid barely moving. She had a sadness to her eyes, which made me love her even more.

She was three years older than me, four grades higher. Her name was Francesca, and I once heard someone call her Frankie. And, well, no one seemed to know anything about her.

Most of us had a story, a history of some sort or the other. You know, our life before…here. Some told, some lied, some were silent, but we all knew something bad had happened to each and all. Besides my aching heart, she gave me something—something that changed my life. But she never knew it.

CHAPTER 3

My first home clung to the edge of a cliff. I'm told it was a red brick, three unit, with us in the middle. It—along with two other ramshackle houses—looked in grave danger of being blown over the steep hill with the next high wind, so the rent was low.

I have only one memory there. Of standing at a window, looking way, way down to a football field below. It was so far down that the kids playing football looked like tiny ants running all around confused and stuff. And if that wasn't enough, just below the kids, tiny cars about to crash into the tiny ants kept disappearing and reappearing. I had fun watching my fascinating world below, and in later years I thought it must have all been a dream. But it wasn't. Our cliff house soared high above the football field that tops New York City's Lincoln Tunnel.

I was born Grant Howard Olsen on a snowy January night. Two weeks later, they changed my name to Robert when my dad had a falling out with his best friend, Grant. I joined Willie, seven; Jeannie, five; and Tom, two. Our sister, Rita, given away at birth. The old man didn't want any more kids, let alone another girl.

I don't know why they kept me, but there I was—my crib snugly tight between three small mattresses on the floor in the back room.

In her later years, my mother would talk about a lot of places, but she would never talk about the house on the cliff.

CHAPTER 4

One morning, Mother woke us before dawn. Out of nowhere, we were moving away. I felt our excitement as we loaded the car with our mother's dishes and pots and a few laundry baskets full of clothes. Our father told us we were going on a *grand adventure*. We were going to "live on the top of a mountain." For such an exciting prospect, our mother remained uncharacteristically quiet the whole drive there.

As we left the city in the early morning hours, we kids quickly fell back to sleep. Somebody yelled "cows!" and I woke up to a new world: rolling green hills dotted with little white farms, fields of cows and horses, faraway tractors surrounded by swirling clouds of white dust. We kids joined our mother's silence, as we squeezed our heads together out the back windows, trying to imagine our new home.

Up and up the mountain we went, until Dad pulled into the drive of a small, red brick house. It was one of only five houses in a row, just a few feet apart, at the very top where the dirt road ended. Curiously, there were two churches up there too. I learned

THE MAST FAMILY FARM.

later they were called "the twin churches," their little white steeples shooting up into the bluest sky. A tiny neighborhood high above the world.

We kids pushed past Dad into the house as he unlocked the door, eager to see what was inside. I remember our thrill at a TV in a cabinet, but our hearts sank when nothing but static filled the small screen. There were only a lumpy green sofa and a couple of chairs in the front room, but the house had three bedrooms! "You and Jeannie take the small bedroom," Mom declared. I didn't mind. It sure was better than all of us kids stuck together like before.

We all helped unload Dad's car. Then he drove away, not helping Mom at all. I heard him return after we had gone to bed.

It was late summer when we arrived, still hot enough to beg for a hose and sprinkler. Mom said no, but the kids in the third house invited us down to cool off in their small plastic pool. Their parents were not home, but the girl was bossy like a mom. Jeannie adored her. The girl only had little brothers, so she would dress Jeannie up in her old clothes and swimsuits, and fashion her hair something fancy.

The fun lasted only a few days. Willie was not one to listen to pool rules, so we soon were banned from their yard. Late that night, Willie and Tom slashed the pool bottom. In the morning the girl showed up at our door, but as usual, our mother denied *her boys* had anything to do with this transgression.

Now Jeannie would take to wandering off down the mountain, chasing this and that, throwing Mother into a panic. We would all be sent out to find her, but we knew where she was. At the Mennonite farm, in the barn, with the horse. Jeannie loved that broken-down mare. I know it was a mare, because the farmer told me.

"Need me a filly," he said, "not this old mare." I didn't know what a filly or mare was, and it sure looked like a horse to me!

Like the girl with the pool, the Mennonites didn't seem to mind retarded people. They were kind-as-all-get-out to Jeannie, whose brain had fried like an egg on hot pavement when no one noticed her burning up with fever one night in the cliff house.

I guess Mom tired of chasing Jeannie, 'cause one day she tied her to the wash line. Jeannie seemed content enough, building little bug houses out of leaves. However, she must have tired of the wash line tether—one day wiggling out of it, along with her dress, and heading right down the mountain to the Mennonites, naked as a baby bird. This time, the farmer's wife brought her home, wrapped in a towel and smiling big time. Back in the city, the social services lady would have come too, but we soon learned nobody cared too much about child welfare on the mountain.

Our father was not around much, sometimes not coming home for days. It was OK with me, because it meant less yelling in the house. Mother took to lying on the sofa more, sometimes forgetting to make dinner, but always drinking beer when she had some.

One day I spotted Willie and Tom slowly rolling something up the mountain. Something big. It was an enormous tractor tire! They yelled at me to come help push, and the three of us got it to the top. Of course with me being the lightest, I had to try it first.

"Get in there, Robbie!" Willie ordered. "You won't fall out if you brace your legs against the other side, and hold on tight!"

I did as I was told, climbed in, secured my position, yelled "ready!" and held my breath. Tom and Willie ran alongside a few seconds to steady the tire, then let go as it got away from them, gaining speed.

I was already so dizzy by the time they let go that it stopped being fun, and I quickly changed my mind. Round and round I went, flying and bumping until we hit a bush and the tire flipped on its side and came to a rest. I dared to open my eyes, saw I was in one piece, and heard my brothers yelling and laughing as they ran down to rescue me. They pulled me out and made me stand up, continuing the fun as I tried to walk normally.

They were next, and soon all agreed that no one felt very good after a spin down the mountain. I refused to go again, and the old tire became a sandbox for Jeannie.

Summer ended, and off to school went Willie and Tom. I wouldn't be six until January, and Mom said half-day kindergarten was a waste, so I played with Jeannie most days.

One day, a man came up the mountain in an old, black car. Everything was black, even the mirrors and bumpers. We never had any visitors, so this was a big deal. But the bigger deal was who drove up next—the sheriff! The black-car man waited for the sheriff to get out first, then slowly opened his door and stepped out. The man in the black car was a Mennonite. All the Mennonites' cars were black.

The sheriff told us kids to go play out back—which we didn't do, following the pair of men to the front door instead. He knocked kinda loud until Mom came to the door, holding her housecoat tightly at her neck. At first she refused to let the men in, then told us kids to go play and opened the door. When they finally left, we ran to see what had happened. But Mom was already in her room with the door locked.

• • • • •

Snow came early to the mountain. I always felt cold, even in the house. I asked Mom for boots, but she wrapped our sneakers in plastic bags and tied string around our ankles instead. I felt bad for Willie. Tom got Willie's old winter coat, I got Tom's, and Jeannie's still fit, but Mom said there was no money for a new one for Willie. He took to wearing Dad's old, thin Army jacket, miles too big.

Our father left every morning early, sometimes before I woke up. No one talked about where he went and what he was doing all day. Before we had moved here, our father had driven a bus, but I didn't think he did that anymore. We never seemed to have any money for stuff and quickly learned not to ask. But that never stopped us from having fun.

One day, Willie and Tom came home from school with a hood from an old Buick they'd found at the junkyard. The perfect giant sled! We turned it upside down, and I sat smack in the middle with Jeannie between my legs. There was nothing to hold unto, so I pressed my feet hard against the hood, holding Jeannie tight. Willie and Tom bent their bodies low to the ground, grabbed on, and pushed as they ran to get a good start—jumping on each side at the last second before the homemade sled took off. Off we flew, down the mountain, the four of us hootin' and hollarin' like wild animals. *This worked way better than that old tractor tire!*

Winters were harsh on the mountain, and sometimes my brothers didn't have school. Our father was home more too—distant and irritable, missing work or wherever he went every morning, unable to navigate the mountain road with those old tires.

Another snowstorm hit. I sat in the back of Dad's car with my brothers next to me, Jeannie in the front seat. I have no idea why we were out in the storm, especially because our father never took us anywhere with him. But there we were.

Dad suddenly lost control of the car, and it spun before coming to rest on a large snowbank. Willie and Tom started laughing, so I joined in—at least until Dad turned around and began punching any one of us that he could reach, taking his frustration out on whoever was near, as usual. We all tried to protect ourselves with our arms over our heads as Dad's face got redder and his blows got harder. He only stopped when Tom's ear started bleeding.

Tom didn't cry or say a word. He never did, refusing to show weakness to our father.

Dad made us all get out of the car, then left us there. *Punishment for laughing,* I guessed.

Jeannie lost a shoe as we were forced out into the snow, so Willie carried her as she sobbed the whole time and wouldn't stop until she got too cold to cry anymore. Willie shaking uncontrollably in his thin jacket, we all walked home in the bitter cold.

No one mentioned the incident again, and in the morning, our father was gone.

Then life changed, up on the mountain.

CHAPTER 5

I realized years later that my father had moved us all to the mountain to leave us there, never to return. It had been his plan all along.

I found out from Willie, who ran into our father many years later, that after he abandoned us, he got a job on a cruise ship. *A cruise ship!* He traveled the world with his handsome self, teaching ballroom dance on the Incres Liner Victoria. Funny, I don't ever remember my dad dancing, but when Willie showed me a photo album of my handsome father in a tuxedo swirling around the dance floor with several attractive women, then I knew the story was true.

Tucked into the album was a colorful brochure describing:

The sublimely elegant white Yacht of the Incres Lines, the luxurious MS Victoria, one of the most popular cruise ships! Directly aft of the magnificent Roman Restaurant is the very large Galley, for the meals on board the Victoria were second to none, the cuisine famed everywhere, for only the finest Beluga caviar would be served with the highest-grade meat

MY HANDSOME FATHER TEACHING DANCE ON THE OCEAN LINER VICTORIA.

and fish, and the salmon the finest Alaskan flown in. The finest truffles, cheeses, and olives would be at hand to create meals that would be spoken about for years to come!

I thought of my father, one of those happy people in the photos, eating all that yummy food. All while Mom was struggling to feed us kids. She had no car, no job, and no money. I was just six but can only imagine now, years later, my mother's shattered heart.

Our food soon ran out, and if it weren't for the kindness of the Mast family down the mountain, we would have starved to death. My mother was much too proud to ask for help, but Jeannie wasn't. One day, she headed down the mountain to the Mennonites and told them that we had no food and she was hungry. Mrs. Mast and the oldest daughter soon arrived, holding Jeannie's hand—and two baskets full of eggs, potatoes, tomatoes, and corn bread. They continued to feed us, and I even remember once sitting around a large dining table at their farmhouse, bowls of steaming food being carried out of the kitchen by their pretty daughters.

One morning, Mom woke us early. With no money for rent, we had to leave our mountain home. Jeannie sat piggyback on Willie as we walked, each of us carrying what we could in pillowcases and grocery bags, down the mountain. No one said much, but I was scared.

In the late afternoon, we came upon a shed. "Probably an old chicken coop," Mom said, and we set up for the night. Tom and Willie gathered sticks to make a small fire with Mom's cigarette lighter, and I could tell Mom was trying to make it into an adventure as we held hotdogs on a branch over our little fire.

We settled in as best we could with the blankets Tom had carried. The back of the shed was open to a forest, with tall pines reaching up into a sky lit with a billion stars. I moved closer to Mom and placed my arm around her. I could feel her tummy move with each slow breath, and I wondered. About Rita, my sister I never knew. I wondered where she was. If she looked like me. I wondered if Mom ever thought about her. If Mom was sorry. If she ever loved Rita. If one day Mom would find her and bring her home.

• • • • •

In the morning, we finished the loaf of bread, spread with a can of something called "C rations" you opened with a little metal twist tab. "Thanks to Uncle Sam," Mom said. We packed up and walked the rest of the way into town.

WELCOME TO FLEETWOOD, HOME OF FISHER BODY. What a sight we must have been! But Mom, defiant even in her grief, dropped us off at a little park with instructions to stay together and not talk to anyone—"especially the police." She returned a few hours later with a jar of Jiffy, more bread, and a key to a two-room furnished apartment above a bar called Arlene and Ray's.

Arlene was a little firecracker of a lady with too much lipstick and too little hair, but kind as all get-out. Her husband, Ray, was a quiet man, tall as Arlene was short, thin-shouldered with a thick head of black hair and glasses that made him look more like a teacher than a barman. Seemed like everyone adored them both.

The deal was Mom would clean the bar every morning and wash dishes in the afternoon in exchange for rent. We boys would go to school together, and Jeannie would hang with Mom.

It was fun living above a bar. Jeannie and I would watch out the front picture window at the people coming and going. We got to know the regulars, the troublemakers, the sad ones, the ones in love. It was funny seeing people check their pockets for money before they went in—or comb their hair, or open their compact and put even more lipstick on. We felt like spies on a secret mission. Well, I did anyway, and Jeannie always went along.

The only not-fun part about living above a bar was that Mom was drinking even more. To her credit, she would never have a drink until she was done with her work tasks. But after five, she could always be found at her favorite stool at the end of the counter having a few. Sometimes Arlene would have to remind her saying, "The kids need dinner. Why don't you run upstairs quickly and feed them?"

I didn't mind Mom being gone, really. After school, it was mostly just me and Jeannie anyway, and I'd make us a sandwich and a glass of powdered milk.

Tom and Willie were not home much either, sometimes not showing up until dark. I missed them more than Mom.

When Jeannie was about eleven, she pulled a chair up to the cupboard and took four pennies from the change jar. She walked down to Arnold's Hardware and bought a piece of bubblegum from the cannister at the cash register. Jeannie forgot to put the money jar back, and Mom soon discovered that the four cents were missing, as every penny was precious in our house. And NO ONE got into Momma's change jar.

Mom lined us kids up in a row and made us open our mouths so she could look for evidence. Yes, Jeannie was a retard, but she wasn't dumb. She hid the gum under her tongue. No culprit was found that day. However, the next morning, Jeannie woke to a tangled mess of hair and Hubba Bubba, as she had fallen asleep with the contraband still in her mouth!

• • • • •

One day we awoke to a man sleeping on Mom's sofa. He was snoring so loudly that Jeannie and I couldn't stop giggling and woke the man up. Trouble is, we laughed even more when we saw his hair going every which way—and that he was in his underpants! I guess he didn't like us giggling, 'cause he reached out and slapped me so hard I fell down, all without even getting off the sofa. Then he turned over and went back to sleep.

Jeannie started crying, so I grabbed her arm, and we ran out the door lest the man would wake up and hit Jeannie too. Still in our pajamas, we hung out in the back stairwell, waiting a long time until we heard the man going down the front stairs and out the front door. Then we bolted out the back door and peeked around the corner just in time to see him drive away in an old pickup truck.

I found out that the man who had slapped me was Jack, Mom's new boyfriend. I also found out that he liked to hit people. Especially Mom.

I'd hear them come upstairs from the bar late at night, talking loudly and laughing. Then I'd hear them doing private stuff—stuff the older boys in the neighborhood always whispered about. Tom told Jeannie and me to put pillows over our heads and go back to sleep, but it was hard with only a curtain between our rooms. Some nights they would fight so bad that Tom and I would climb out the window and hang in the alley until they stopped—or until they just fell asleep. We'd always first move Jeannie under her bed for safekeeping before we left, but mercifully Jack seemed to leave her alone.

• • • • •

There was a paper-box factory behind Arlene and Ray's—a red brick building with Fleetwood Box Company painted in white across the front. I loved that place. We could hear the hum of the machines from our back window, and well, the mystery and excitement were just too much—so I had to see what they were doing in there.

As soon as I got home from school, I would run over, pull a couple of crates under the factory window in the back of the building, climb up, and watch the man load a stack of thick paper into the large machine. I'd watch as the machine would then cut it into perfect rectangles with little flaps on one side. Then the man would run to the other end and fold the rectangles into perfect, little, white, shirt boxes —one after the other—then stack them up a dozen high.

There was another man in there, too. He was always in a small room in the corner, and I could only see him from the window on the other side. One day that man suddenly was standing in the parking lot behind me, but I didn't know it until he spoke and scared the bejeebers out of me. I jumped down and started to run, but he spoke softly and said, "Please wait, son. You are not in trouble." Something about him made me pause, but I still stayed far away, able to escape if needed.

He asked if I might like to help out a little. Maybe sweep the floor and empty the trash cans. I started to calm down, and then couldn't believe my luck. He was offering me another job! I was usually done helping Ray the milkman by seven on Saturdays, and I could work every day after school if need be.

I found out his name was Mr. Rosenburg, and he had a nice wife. She was pretty and wore fancy hats with duck feathers and smelled good and would bring him lunch sometimes.

I loved the box factory. The rhythm of those cutting machines, the smell of paper freshly cut, the neatly stacked boxes—I had never seen anything like it.

One day, Lenny, the man who ran the machines, asked if I'd like to ride in the truck and help with deliveries. *Boy would I.*

Lenny kept a candy stash in the glove box and always let me help myself to as much as I wanted. I felt important helping to load something called a "dolly," pushing it up to the back doors and ringing the little delivery bell.

On Saturdays, Mrs. Rosenburg started bringing lunch for me too. My favorite was a noodle pudding with cinnamon, and these little white balls with a spicy red sauce on top. She said it was fish, but it sure didn't look like a fish to me.

I never told Mom about the delicious food. She always said we "didn't need no help from nobody," and I was afraid she might find out where I went every day after school and mess the whole thing up.

When the boys were home, it seemed like Willie would pick a fight with Mom about everything. He was so mad all the time. His anger just steamed off his body like a street pothole in winter. Tom had told about Jack smacking me, and Willie swore, "if Jack ever hits you or anyone again, I'll fucking kill him. For real!"

A short time later, Willie dropped out of ninth grade and took to the streets like a wild dog. I missed him, but Mom hardly noticed he was gone.

One day, Mom came home with news: she had gotten a better job as custodian of our school.

Once she started working at the school, I liked seeing her in the hallway sometimes. We would wave. But Tom said it was embarrassing—our mom cleaning the toilet rooms.

Mom started buying us little things with her extra money. A tiny fairy doll for Jeannie and a model car kit for me. Tom got a new shirt, because he was always complaining about wearing Willie's old ones.

The only bad part about having more money was Mom staying even later at the bar. We tucked ourselves in most nights.

One day after school, Willie stopped by. I was thrilled. I loved Willie. He was almost like a rock star to me. I was still a scrawny little guy with thick glasses and funny hair, but no one messed with me when Willie was around. Seemed like the whole neighborhood was afraid of him. He swung me up on his back and ran around the front room, both of us laughing like crazy, and of course Jeannie had to be next.

Mom wasn't as happy to see him though. He told Mom he needed to talk to her, and they went into the back room and soon started arguing. They got louder and angrier. I should have taken Jeannie outside, but I didn't. They were really going at it, when all of a sudden, we heard a really loud thud—and then nothing.

Willie flew out of the room and down the stairs. Still no sound.

"Mom, you OK? Mommy?" I called. Jeannie and I peeked into the room to find our mother on the floor, blood everywhere. Next to her lay Tom's baseball bat.

Willie had hit our mother over the head with that bat. I must have been in shock, or maybe it was just too horrible to take in, but it seemed like we stood there for the longest time.

Finally, I turned to Jeannie, who had buried her face in her sweater. "Run downstairs quick and get an adult. Anybody! Now!"

I knelt down next to my mother, her hair matted in blood. "Mom?" She didn't answer, but she was still breathing.

Soon all hell broke loose—police sirens, ambulances, people all over our apartment taking pictures and yelling stuff. Someone picked Jeannie and me up and carried us downstairs into the arms of a sobbing Arlene.

I felt better when Tom later showed up. "Do not to tell the police anything," he whispered to me and Jeannie. But they already knew who to look for. Willie had spent more time in jail than out, and he was only fifteen.

In a few hours, we kids were in the custody of social services. "You are all going to be fine now," the lady said. "You will be coming with me." Then she bent down and looked right at Jeannie. "Hmmm, we'll see about you too." I didn't like the sound of that.

We were told our mother may not live, but that we were going to a safe place.

Tom and I were taken miles away from Fleetwood to The Children's Home of Reading, and poor Jeannie even further away to the Home for the Retarded near Philadelphia. We boys would spend five months at the orphanage, but it wouldn't be our last visit. Little did we know that our sweet, beautiful, kind, and funny Jeannie would never come home.

FLEETWOOD, PENNSYLVANIA

THE OLD PAPER BOX FACTORY

LEFT: ABOVE ARLEEN AND RAY'S BAR. JEANNIE, ME AND TOMMY.

BELOW: ARLEEN AND RAY'S BAR. NOW HOMER'S BAR, FLEETWOOD, PENNSYLVANIA.

Willie, being a minor at fifteen, would spend twenty-two months in a lockdown, prison-like, juvenile detention center. *Getting angrier by the day.*

CHAPTER 6

I don't remember a lot about our first time at The Children's Home. I read once that when you are scared, your memory kind of shuts down. I guess that happened to me.

Plus I was only ten, and nobody remembers much about being ten.

Funny thing though. I do perfectly remember the day we arrived there, and the day we left.

I missed Jeannie terribly and was glad they let Tom sleep in bed with me the first night. In the morning, we had to get up early, tidy our beds, and wash up in the large lavatory with the other boys. No one talked to us, as we watched the others to see what to do. There was a long wall of small sinks. Tom and I found two that were free, and washed up quickly. When we got back to our sleeping room, our own clothes were gone, but there were pants, shirts, undies, and socks that were not ours folded neatly on our beds. I looked at Tom, he shrugged, and we put them on.

I was starving but too afraid to ask about food, when a bell rang and the other boys flew out of the dorm and down the stairs to breakfast. Tom and I followed and got in a line with the others. When we got close to the serving area, we saw cereal in a large container; we saw that we would put our bowls under, and then pull a lever. We soon learned why the boys were filling their bowls so high, catching the overflow in their shirttails, not leaving much room for milk. We each only got one bowl, so if we were hungry, we had to fill it to the brim on our one trip to the dispenser.

There were girls in there too, but they stayed on the other side of the dining hall and had their own cereal dispenser.

Tom and I didn't go to school with the rest of the boys that day. We had to see a nurse upstairs on the third floor, where I refused to take my underwear off. I started scanning the room for a possible open window. I knew we were high up, but thought I could make it to the roof and find a way down from there if she wouldn't stop trying to get me to undress. But she did—letting me keep my underwear on, but looking under my arms and everything else real good. Tom gave her a harder time, so she said his exam could wait a day.

I thought we would be going to our regular school, not realizing we were now in a different city. I soon learned we would be attending Riverside Elementary, and I soon learned something else too. That we stood out. And not in a good way. We were the kids from THE HOME.

I hated school. I did my best to be invisible. Thankfully assigned to the back row, I had frequent neck aches from keeping my head down.

Tom, not so much, when it came to being invisible. He was a frequent visitor to the headmaster's office, and soon was getting into fights at the Home too. He was moved out of my dormitory to join the teen boys, even though he was just twelve.

I missed my mom, especially at night since Tom no longer slept next to me. And I wondered what Jeannie was doing, far away in Philadelphia, wherever that was. I thought about Willie too. I knew he would be OK. Everyone said he was crazy in the eyes, and nobody messed with him because of it. Still, I wondered if he was sorry, and if he missed me.

The days became weeks, the weeks became months—winter coming and going, along with my eleventh birthday.

Then one day, out of nowhere, Tom and I were going home.

Mom hadn't died after all, but had sobered up in the hospital. Ray and Arlene had had enough and rented our apartment to someone else. "You won't be going back to your old neighborhood," said the social worker lady. I thought about my job at the box factory. I never had a chance to tell them what had happened, and I hoped they didn't find a new boy while I was gone.

Thanks to programs like Aid to Families with Dependent Children (AFDC) and food stamps, Mom was able to find an old trailer to move into. The social worker lady said, "As long as you kids have a place to sleep and food in the cupboard, your mom can take you home." Mom had those things for us, so home we went.

But Jeannie never came home. Mom just left her there. In Philadelphia. In an adult sanitarium. I wasn't even allowed to talk about her. I wouldn't see my sister for ten years.

• • • • •

Our trailer was in a whole new part of town, so I had some research to do on where things were. I had to find a hardware store for sure, so I could find parts for the rocket I designed in my dreams at the Home. But I guessed that didn't matter until I earned some money again. Mom said there was no milkman in this place, and the box factory was on the other side of town, so I would have to think of something else to keep myself employed.

Tom came home one day with a BB gun. I knew he hadn't bought it; nobody had any money. When I asked him about it, he said he found it; but I knew he hadn't. He had stolen it for sure.

Sometimes he let me go with him down to the creek to shoot fish. We never got any, but it was fun anyway.

One day when Tom was gone, I took the gun. I slid it down into my pants and walked kinda stiff-legged out of the trailer and down to the creek. I shot a few times into the water, then sat down on the soft grass and threw a few pieces of bread from my pocket into the creek to see what might come up. A little movement across the creek caught my eye. A turtle! I thought it was a snapper, since its head pointed a bit. Still, he was a bit small for a snapper. I watched him for a while, enjoying his nap on a fallen branch. I picked up the gun, lifted the little sight to my eye, aimed, and I shot him.

I saw his little body fly somewhere up on the bank, and then go quiet. Only the gentle sound of the creek kept me company as the weight of what I had done suddenly pressed hard upon my heart.

I put my head in my hands, shut my eyes tight, and I cried. I sobbed. I wailed. And then I cried more. My whole body shook with grief at my actions.

When I had nothing left, I got up and crossed the creek.

He wasn't a snapper, but a perfect little painted turtle. My BB stuck deep in his beautiful shell. I prayed he was just stunned, as I ever so slowly brought him up to my face to see. But he was so still. I laid him back down on the grass, my face resting next to his.

"I'm sorry. I'm so, so sorry."

When I was sure he was never going to wake up, I took off my shirt and wrapped him ever so gently. I found a stick and started digging a little grave for him next to a small tree on the bank, so I would always be able to visit him. I stayed there, holding vigil, until it got too dark. Then I got up and walked home.

“There is another world, but it is in this one.”

—Paul Eluard

CHAPTER 7

I live in a pine forest. The kind where the trees are lined up in perfect rows, one after the other, as far as the eye can see. There is no shrubbery or weeds, not even a forest fern. Only soft pine needles and small pools of sunlight blanketing my forest floor.

And it's so quiet. That's my favorite part. The silence. I can't even hear our neighbor Kenny's enormous car stereo that he blasts every afternoon from our trailer park that lines the forest edge.

I lay on the soft ground sometimes with my hands behind my head and look up at the night sky—watching for shooting stars through the trees above. No one ever comes looking for me, but if they did, they would never find me—my tree house home disappearing into the thick, high branches of my forest canopy.

I decide it still needs some work. My tree house. I will soon replace the tar paper roof with a piece of corrugated fiberglass I found at the dump. This will surely keep me dry and let the moonlight shine through a bit. I also found a better hinge for my trap door, but I'll have to go back to the dump with some tools to remove it from that old cabinet. My bucket pulley system works great, although I can't put too many supplies in it at once, as my arms get too tired hauling it up so high. I use sticks to prop open my bark-slab window coverings, weather permitting, and I sleep well in my hammock made from an old paint tarp. I even have a Tarzan rope swing, but I have to pull it up through the trap door when not in use, so as not to leave even a tiny hint of my secret hideaway above.

The forest animals are my friends, and I never get lonesome for people. The forest will tell me things if I stay very still and listen to it. I learned that birds can feel the coming of storms and strangers, and that smaller animals are almost in a tizzy when the sky darkens and the winds change.

Once on the TV show, *Tarzan,* when the village was under attack, the people climbed up into the tree houses and pulled the ropes up behind them. If their enemies tried to chop down the trees and set them on fire, they would be pelted with rocks and spears from the treetops.

I suppose I could make some spears, and the creek has plenty of rocks. But I really don't think I'd need them. Nobody has come around. However, my trap door does have that new dead bolt I found at the junkyard, and a quick kick would close it without too much effort.

I should have gotten a longer rope. Since I knotted it every three feet, it is a bit short, so I have to climb with only my hands at first, pulling my feet from the earth, then continuing hand over hand, both feet jumping to the next knot. My arms are getting stronger as I practice pulling the rope up faster and faster. I wish I had one of those stopwatches so I could time myself.

The creek is my water source, and if I run out of food, I fish and collect wild berries. I'm happy here, all by myself, living among the birds, far away from the world.

That's my plan anyway—when I save enough to buy some wood, nails, rope, and stuff. And I'll have to save enough for food too. For now, I'll just be happy no one follows me here after school, and the supplies I've collected so far are still in my special spot, hidden under the fallen tree root.

I once heard a story on Mom's radio of a fisherman who spent years building a tree house on the edge of a redwood forest by the sea. His son had drowned when their boat was wrecked on a rocky shore during a terrible storm. After his boy's death, the man began collecting driftwood—odd pieces of this and that brought by the tide, and fallen redwood branches. Near madness in his grief, one could find him at all hours, even night, hammering away at his treetop memorial in the moonlight.

His tree house soon became a favorite hangout for the neighborhood children. He had even created a kind of wishing well of sorts, somehow hauling an old birdbath halfway up the tree and securing it on its own little platform. The children could make a wish, then try like crazy to get their penny to land inside the bowl so their dreams would come true.

I heard that the man died one day, but his boy's treetop tribute still stands, weathered and unstable, reaching up toward heaven.

Sometimes I dream about that boy—that he didn't drown after all, but wandered the woods until he heard his father's hammer high in the treetops. He followed the sound until he found his dad, and they lived happily ever after, high in their treetop paradise.

• • • • •

Hey, did you know that pine trees are magical? Yep, it's true. And did you know that pine trees emit something called "phytoncides"? I didn't either. But I should have. They are a kind of pheromone that makes people better. For real. Of course I didn't find this out 'til I was older, but it sure explains a lot. I always felt better in the forest.

They call it "forest bathing," and doctors in Japan tell people they need to do it. Even if they're not sick. Walking slowly is the way to go, they say, and it will reduce stress, anxiety, depression, and even anger. Turns out there is more oxygen in forests too, and that makes people even happier!

I wished Willie wasn't in juvie and could breathe in some of that forest air, even though I didn't yet know about those phytoncides.

All this was discovered in the 1980s, so I sure was way ahead of those scientists. I probably could have discovered some new forest stuff about feelings and chemicals and such and become famous—had we not been taken away to the orphanage again. My dream had to wait, and it would be years before I could return to my forest hideaway.

CHAPTER 8

Mom found a new bar that she could walk to from the trailer, so Tom and I were alone again most nights. Sometimes Tom would go out too, but he would never let me come along with him, no matter how much I begged.

And I missed Jeannie, often dreaming of her alone in that place for the retarded, so far away.

One moonless night in late summer when Tom and Mom were both gone and I had tucked myself in, I woke to Willie standing next to my bed. He was out of juvie, but Mom had refused to let him come home.

"Get up, Robbie. I need your help." I sat up, rubbing the sleep from my eyes. "Hurry up! And put on dark clothes. No white socks!!!"

You would always do what Willie told you to. I felt a small thrill inside. *My big brother needs me.*

We headed out in the darkest of nights, hunched over, stepping quietly, avoiding the streetlights, making our way through the back alleys and across railroad tracks. I would never come to this area on my own, and I still didn't know where we were going or why. Every time I tried to ask, Willie whispered impatiently, "Shut up, Robbie; just follow me!" He carried a large duffle bag, and I thought maybe we were going to collect soda bottles and turn them in for green stamps, but that didn't make much sense. We couldn't see very well at night.

I was getting tired but didn't want to tell Willie, so I tried to keep up; and pretty soon we stopped across the street from a big, fancy house, ducking into some low bushes. We stayed there for a few minutes, then he reached into his duffle bag and handed me a large whistle.

"Now listen, Robbie, if you see a car pull into the driveway of that house across the street, or if anybody comes around, you blow that whistle as hard as you can, and then run back to the railroad tracks and wait for me there. You understand?"

I understood. We were stealing. *Robbing houses.* So this must be what Willie and his friends had been doing at night. Playing Robin Hood, but for real. "Nothin' wrong with it, Robbie. Taking from the rich and giving to the poor—us!"

I didn't have to blow the whistle that night or any night. Willie seemed to disappear into the night like a ghost. Sometimes he would appear next to me in the bushes out of thin air, his duffle so heavy we both had to carry it home.

One moonless night, we headed out together as usual, but this time Willie bent down and looked in my face, his hands so tight on my shoulders it hurt. "You are coming inside with me this time, Robbie, and you will do exactly what I tell you to." I wasn't sure how I felt about this. I liked being his lookout, but this was different. What if I made a mistake and fell inside, or got trapped or bitten by a dog? No, I didn't like this at all. But Willie insisted, so I went along.

Willie must have been inside the house before. He knew what window was left unlocked, hiked me up into the house, and pulled himself in after me. He grabbed my arm, and we tiptoed up a wide, dark stairway to the second floor. We stopped to listen, then we continued down a long hall to a large bedroom. Willie turned on a tiny flashlight, and we crossed the room and entered a smaller room with perfectly lined-up clothes and shoes on three walls, and a whole cabinet of drawers on the other. In the middle of the room was a fancy chair with fringe. I had never seen anything like it. Willie opened a lower cabinet and flashed his light on a small safe with a combination lock on the front. "I can't carry this alone, Robbie, so you are going to help me. You get that end and pull hard." There was just enough room around the safe to slide my fingers around the corners, and I pulled as hard as I could; but it was so heavy that Willie's side came out first, and it got stuck. Willie tried to push his side back in, but that seemed to make matters worse. No matter how we tried, it was just wouldn't budge.

Willie started getting mad, and I begged to leave lest the rich people come home. But Willie said, "We ain't leavin' with nothin'," and told me to check the bedrooms across the hall. "Go to the dresser and look on top for any cash or jewelry," he commanded. "Then open the first drawer and feel for stuff under clothes, and check the bedside tabletops—and be sure not to go near any windows. Now hurry!"

Once on Mom's favorite TV show, *The Avengers,* a thief dressed in a black catsuit used a laser gun to burn through the lock on a large safe to steal the world's largest diamond. Then he opened a window, threw out a line, and scaled down a tall skyscraper—jumping into the open roof of a fancy car and speeding away into the night.

Sure wish I had one of those laser guns so Willie wouldn't be mad at me about not being able to move the safe. I heard Willie whisper my name, and it snapped me back into action. I grabbed a watch and some rings from a little bowl on the dresser. I never got to the other rooms, with Willie grabbing my arm angrily and pulling me down the steps, not even trying to be quiet. We climbed out the window and ran like mad into the darkness.

• • • • •

One morning, we woke up to a man in our trailer. He was sleeping in Mom's bed, snoring so bad I was sure he would wake himself up. I tiptoed to Mom's room and pulled back the curtain. *Jack had found us.*

"Get dressed quick Robbie, and be quiet!" Tom whispered, and we tiptoed out and ran to school without breakfast, not wanting to make a sound lest Jack wake up. I was worried all day and didn't go home after school, hanging at the playground until it got too dark. When I got near the trailer, I could hear Jack and Tom going at it. *I was afraid this might happen.* Tom had told me he was tired of Jack smacking us around and Mom doing nothing about it.

I heard Tom telling Jack to "get out of our house" or he would call the police. Jack stopped arguing, and I thought he might actually leave. I peeked in the window and saw Jack smile a little, but then he smacked Tom across the face so hard that Tom fell back into the kitchen table. This time, Tom couldn't hold back his tears and ran out the trailer door, holding his stinging face.

I caught up to him, and we ran together until I thought my lungs would explode. "Slow down," I begged Tom. He could hardly look at me, ashamed that he cried, I think.

No matter how hard our father would hit us when we were little, Tom never cried. "Never show weakness, Robbie," he always said. But this time was different. Tom seemed different, and it scared me.

He did what he said he was going to do. We walked almost an hour into town and found the police station. The front door was locked, so Tom pounded on it, and a policeman came and let us come inside. I saw his expression change when he saw the red welts on Tom's face. He got us both a 7-Up out of the soda machine with his own money and told us to "wait here." He soon returned with another man who had a tie on and didn't look like a policeman. "I'm Detective Johnson. Boys, I want you to tell me what happened, and don't be afraid. Just tell me the truth; I'm here to help you."

The police drove us home, and thankfully Jack was gone. They told us to wake our mother up, then go to our room so they could talk to her in private. We heard them talking to Mom, but they kept their voices down so we couldn't hear what they were saying. After a while, they left, and Mom went back to bed without a word.

• • • • •

On an unusually quiet evening at the trailer, I was working on a design sketch for a model rocket I planned to build. Tom was out somewhere, and Mom was on the couch nursing a hangover when Jack busted in, mad as all get-out. Now the only way out of the trailer was to walk through where Jack was standing, so I ran to the back bedroom. There was no door into the room; only a thin curtain hung between Jack and me. I climbed onto the small dresser, opened the window above it as quietly as I could, and jumped out.

One foot landed wrong on a broken cement block that Tom had put there so he could climb back in at night when Mom locked him out. It turns out, I broke my ankle.

But I didn't yet know it was broken. All I could feel was my racing heart.

I knew I would never make it to the forest, so I crawled a few yards and hid behind the neighbor's doghouse. I tenderly removed my shoe and sock. My ankle was doubling in size, throbbing with pain.

All was quiet for a while, then the trailer door burst open, and I saw Jack pulling Momma down the steps by her hair, dragging her across the yard, then throwing her into the street. To my horror, I saw that my mother was completely naked. Jack then walked calmly to his pickup and drove away.

I did not move. I did not help my mom. My fear of being seen with her by the neighbors was just too much. I stayed hidden, holding my throbbing ankle, and watched my mother pick herself up and go home.

When I was sure Jack wasn't coming back, I scooted on my behind across the yard and into the house. Mom had her bedroom door shut, so I got some ice cubes out of the tray, wrapped them in a towel, laid on the sofa, and iced my foot as best I could—then fell into a deep sleep.

Of course the juicy news spread through the neighborhood like wildfire, and the shame of being an Olsen reared its ugly head again. Tom came home, and no one in the neighborhood said a word to me—frightened of Tom as they were—but I knew what they were thinking. A few days later we woke to the words "white trash" spray painted next to the trailer door.

Eventually my broken ankle was addressed with a cast from my toes to my knee, my mother's hair grew back, and something wonderful happened—but I couldn't tell. I was given crutches to use for six weeks and ordered not to overdo.

Every morning, my mom would open the cupboard under the sink and retrieve the box of Borax. Inside, she stashed her emergency money—of which I was given two precious quarters. It was the first time in my life I could ride the city bus to school.

That is, I was *supposed* to ride the bus to school. Instead, I saw my chance.

Woolworth's Five and Dime was my second favorite hangout. The lunch counter's shiny, red stools swiveled around, and the place smelled like French fries. The hot dogs had square buns, and the Coke had cherry in it. I know 'cause I ate there once with my mom on my birthday. Tom begged to come with us too, but Mom said we didn't have enough money. I felt bad for Tom about that.

I loved to wander down the aisles. The hardware department was my favorite. I dreamed of the cool stuff I could build and was curious about all the gadgets and tools in little brown boxes filling the shelves.

Now I had my two bus quarters! All I had to do was get up early enough to make it to school on my crutches without Mom noticing I didn't get on the bus. I felt as happy as a dog with two tails.

I did the math. It would take eleven and a half days of walking to school with my crutches to have the $5.75 for the rocket kit I was longing for. Then with the cardboard tube and supplies I already had, I could finish my rocket. It was a splendid plan. That is, if my armpits held out—as I was in pain and quite tired by the time I reached school and returned home each day. All went well until a neighbor lady saw me struggling on day five, seven blocks from home, and asked my mother why the hell she wouldn't give me bus money, with a broken foot even!

That ended that. I had to give the money back. I was so upset that I tore up all my rocket designs that I had worked so hard on and threw them at my mother. She picked one up and studied it. "Hmmm…well, would ya look at this. I guess he was right. What he said. That box factory man. That you know stuff beyond your years, that you are quite intelligent. That you should have opportunities……education, blah, blah, blah. Can you believe the nerve?! The gull of those rich people! Thinking they could just adopt you! I showed them the door!"

I just stood there, stunned, staring at my mother—then out the window at a dusky sky, my eyes filling with tears. *They had wanted me.*

Mr. and Mrs. Rosenburg had wanted to adopt me. Had actually found out where I lived and knocked on our door and asked my mom to take me home to their grand house to be their son.

The sky was darkening, clouds moving by quickly. No matter. I grabbed my jacket and a couple of cans of Spam, filled my school Thermos, and ran out the door. I kept running and running, never looking back until I reached the forest edge. Once there, I turned back and looked behind me. No one was coming after me. No one ever did.

I made my way to my hideout in the moonlight, a little fort under a large fallen pine tree's giant roots. I hunkered down for the night, curling up inside myself, falling asleep quickly, dreaming of the life that could have been mine.

Jack came back a few weeks later, and Tom was home this time. Tom was almost fourteen now and had told me he would never let Jack hit us again. He had made a plan weeks ago, although I begged him not to do it.

This time, Jack had brought a bottle of whiskey with him—a

peace offering of sorts, I guess. We stayed in the back room, quiet as church mice, and we waited.

When enough time and whiskey had passed, Tom picked up the metal milk box that he had stashed away, tiptoed out carefully, sneaked up behind our mom and Jack, and hit Jack as hard as he could on the head. Thank God he knocked Jack out, because Tom forgot to plan what he would do next.

Mom screamed something awful, blood was everywhere, and Jack was coming to. Tom yelled, "RUN!" We took off so fast, we probably left smoke behind as we tore off in different directions—me to the forest, and Tom to the old mill.

I wish we would have stayed together. I guessed my brother hadn't thought this out. Even Tom didn't know where my forest hideout was, so he would never find me.

I waited 'til dark, then walked to the mill, ducking when cars went by. I climbed in the window and found Tom asleep on our musty rugs.

A few days later, Mom told us, "Pack a few things, and don't ask questions." I thought maybe Mom was surprising us with a trip to see her Aunt Tilly in New Jersey to make up for Jack hitting us all the time.

Mom, Tom, and I got on the bus, and my heart sunk when we all stepped off at The Children's Home. Mom walked us to the door, told us to go in, turned around, and walked away—without even a *goodbye*.

CHAPTER 9

The Home for Friendless Children 1884–1964.
The Reading Children's Home 1964–1984.

We orphans just called it The Mission.

Tom ran away on our first day back at The Mission. He didn't even ask me to go with him. I would have said no anyway. I was just so tired of worrying about Jack and being hungry all the time. At least here we got three meals a day, even if we misbehaved. Most of the same kids were here, and I soon settled into my old routine.

Tom came back a few days later, hungry and cold, begging to be let in. Every "runner" would get a good paddling and a bunch of extra chores, but that didn't seem to make much of a difference. We had runners all of the time.

I was assigned a different bed from our last time here, and was happy to see it was at the end of the row and next to a window. There were some new boys, so the beds were now only about two feet apart. Being at the end, I only had one boy next to me. *Maybe he will leave me alone, I thought. But* regardless, somehow having the window next to my bed gave me comfort—although I thought I would probably break something in my body again if I tried to jump out of it.

Tom was taken to the third floor with the older boys, so I was left to my own defenses. Even though the punishment was severe for fighting, it never stopped the troublemakers, and we had plenty of them—the boy with one eye being the worst offender.

But I was excited to learn that we now had a TV room! It was pretty small though, maybe 10 by 12 feet—with small, wooden folding chairs pushed up against each other, completely filling the room, save for maybe a foot or so along the walls for aisles. We'd pack in there as tight as a can of sardines, all eyes straining to see the small black-and-white TV set in a small console propped up on four blocks of wood for better viewing.

One hour on Wednesday nights and Saturday mornings were the allowed TV times, but Wednesday was the biggie. We'd wait all week with anticipation for the next *Batman and Robin* episode. I just loved that show. KABOOM! POW! CLASH! BAM! SPLATT! HOLY RAVIOLI! The kids would holler and carry on, until Mrs. Cosenza stuck her head in and threatened to turn off the TV. But I never yelled. I was busy planning the model Batmobile that I would build when I got out of here and went to the Hobby Store on 6th. Well, after I could get another paper route, that is.

I was so happy to find that George the janitor was still here. He was my first real friend at The Mission. Most of the kids were afraid of him. He had a hole in his throat and had to put a finger over it to talk. It must have hurt, because George never said much. When he did, he'd scare the bejeebers out of the kids with the sound he'd make. But it never bothered me much. I used to follow him around the place, curious about the various tools and such he carried in his toolbox. Most I had never seen before. At first I hid when I watched him work on stuff that needed fixing, but one day I just couldn't stand it.

"What are you doing?" I asked.

I was beyond happy when he asked me if I'd like to be his assistant after school—handing him tools and holding the flashlight sometimes. He taught me what a tap was and how to use a level. One Saturday, we went down to the boiler room where George had a large worktable, and we made a birdhouse with wood scraps. We nailed it to the tree near the playground. It had a tiny little hole, and I didn't think any bird could fit through it.

"There is one," George said. "It sings louder than the big birds. Its tiny body trembling at the sound of its own song."

I think George likes me. I never make fun of him like the others, and try hard to be a good assistant. Mr. and Mrs. Cosenza, the orphan keepers who run this place, were not sure about the whole thing. But George said I was a good assistant, so they let the arrangement slide.

• • • • •

One day, I snuck down to the boiler room and shyly asked, "George, could you help me make a slingshot?" I had been searching The Mission's grounds for weeks to find the perfect Y-shaped branch. He smiled and nodded yes. We used a knife to strip off all the bark and rounded all the edges with a rasp to make it super comfortable to hold. We used a handsaw and a file to make grooves so the band wouldn't slip. Then we sanded the whole thing using 220-grit sandpaper. We rubbed oil all over it to "bring out the beauty of the wood," as George described it. Luckily, we found a large rubber band and a small piece of leather we cut to size, poked two holes in, and threaded the bands through. Then we wrapped the band around the deep grooves and tied them securely at the fork ends. It was beautiful, and I was aching to show it off, but George said, "You best keep it hidden."

But I just couldn't. I don't know why, but I told the boy with one eye about the slingshot. I figured that the eye he had left might have super abilities, and I had to see for myself.

I found out his name was Joe, and we made a plan to steal some paper clips from Mr. Cosenza's office whenever someone left the door unlocked. They eventually did, and we did, and off to the library we ran without permission when the playground matron wasn't looking. We hid ourselves behind the low cement wall along the wide front steps and pulled the slingshot from inside my jacket.

From there, we had the perfect perch to shoot our paper clips, taking turns aiming at the unsuspecting pedestrians passing by. It was a blast watching them react to a sharp, sudden sting on a bare arm or leg. I had been right about Joe; he sure was a sharpshooter with that one good eye. If his stepdad hadn't knocked out the other one, he would become a sniper for the Army, he said. We laughed like crazy behind our hidden perch, as our victims jumped and swatted the imaginary bugs away—not sure what had just happened, looking around, then moving on.

We were having such a blast that we didn't notice the policeman coming up the steps behind us. "Shame on you boys!" He scolded. "What if you hit a little old lady?"

"But we ain't aiming at little old ladies!" Joe blurted out. The policeman was not amused. He walked us back to The Mission, and it was the first time I got the paddle—that thing had holes drilled in it! It hurt like heck, but maybe not as much as it might have had my brain not been busy figuring out how its holes affected air flow, drag, aerodynamics, and increased velocity.

One-eyed Joe knew a lot about how things worked around The Mission. One day, I asked him why so many kids were never adopted, myself included. He told me that most of the kids were not "eligible." He said that meant their parents would not "sign off" on them. "So they can never leave here, unless their parents come back to get them—or they just run away," he explained. He told me that once in a while, a parent could come to "visit" their kid.

But my mom never came. I figured she never knew about this option, and I wished I could send her a note. But I had no idea where she was.

Joe told me he thought his mom had come once, years ago. He had a faint memory of a lady in a bright green skirt placing him on her lap. He couldn't remember her face, but he remembered her skirt had safety pins all around the bottom, and one stuck him in the leg! "She never came again," he said.

"The best way out is always through."

—Robert Frost

CHAPTER 10

There were no classrooms at The Mission. We all walked to the local school—some to Riverside Elementary, some to Northwest Junior High. The older kids went to Reading High. But we were all the same, just like last time: *the kids from THE HOME.*

I was a poor student, preferring to sketch the latest rocket design I had been dreaming about, hidden inside my geography book. I had begun to collect more cardboard tubes and pieces of wire I'd find on my way home from school, and I even found the perfect cement block for my launch pad. It was hard sneaking it into The Mission, so I often hid my stash under the porch of the large mansion next door, planning to retrieve it all when I was old enough to leave—or run away with Tom.

• • • • •

I never read a book until I was twelve years old. Nope, not a single one. We never had books, only Mom's Sears and Roebuck catalog. The day of reckoning came in Mrs. Langdon's class. A book report. Now I'd been given lots of book report assignments, starting in first grade, but Olsens didn't do homework.

This was different. You did your homework in The Mission. Period.

We had a small library on the first floor of The Mission. It was down the hall from the "meet and greet if you're lucky room," a wood-paneled parlor that smelled like lemon, with tall heavy curtains and two green velvet love seats facing each other. On a side table was a super fancy silver tea set. I knew this, because Tom told me. He and some older boys had snuck in one day when the door was left unlocked. I made him tell me every little detail he remembered, as I had spent many hours lying in bed, imagining my interview. They would be kind and soft-spoken. She would be pretty and smile a lot, and he would shake my hand and like to build stuff and call me *son*. They always wanted a boy just my age, and could they take me home that day?

Or maybe Mr. and Mrs. Rosenberg would hear I was here and come get me, and I would run the box factory one day after all.

Anyway, back to the library. One of the older kids was working the desk, reading a comic book, and barely noticed me come in.

Our book had to be at least one hundred pages, so the first thing I did was find a one-hundred-page book to see how thick it was. I ran my fingers over the bookends as I walked down the rows, pulling out books matching that size. When I couldn't hold any more books, I sat down at a small desk and piled them on the floor next to me. I picked up each one, giving it a five-second going-over before tossing it in the "no way" pile.

I was just about through them, when one caught my eye. The cover had splashes of red and navy blue, and what looked like a snow-covered mountain peeking out in the distance. Small pine trees were off to the sides, and smack in the middle of this messy collage of color was a perfect little yellow seaplane, taking off over the jagged ice of a small lake. *The Puddle Jumper, the Adventures of a Young Flyer in Alaska,* by Tom E. Clark. I opened the book and read the inside cover.

Arne Peterson's father was one of the best bush pilots in Alaska. Small wonder, then, that young Arne himself was a good pilot and loved to fly his dad's Travel Air. It was always a wonderful sensation to feel the pontoons lift from the water, see the cloud of spray drop astern, and know the "puddle jumper" was airborne.

Well, maybe this wouldn't be so bad, I thought. I quickly turned to the very last page. 91. Close enough. I ran back to my room, jumped under my blanket, found my flashlight, and began reading. I awoke in the morning with crooked glasses, holding The Puddle Jumper close to my heart.

To a fatherless boy, Gunner Peterson was larger than life. Brave, smart, adventurous yet strict, kind, and funny. His motto was "no work—no eat." I'd be fine with that. I liked to do stuff.

Arne and his dad had all kinds of adventures flying bear hunters and the like to Kodiak Island. Sudden changes of weather in Alaska made for some exciting stories. One of my favorites was when Gunner turned the controls over to Arne as the weather quickly changed. "You need to practice flying in this stuff, son," he said.

"OK, it's your airplane." Arne eased the throttle back, and moments later they settled into the fog like a submarine sinking beneath the surface of the sea.

They hauled huge bear hides back to the main island, and once flew through a dangerous snowstorm to pick up an injured hunter. Another time, they even rescued an abandoned horse from a deserted island! But somehow they always made it home in time for Arne's mom's delicious moose stew.

Each night I would read until I couldn't keep my eyes open. When I finished, I'd read the book all over again. Mrs. Langdon said I would have gotten an A on my book report, but for the grammar and spelling.

CHAPTER 11

One week each summer, a large bus would come to pick us up for a week at Camp Joy, about an hour's drive from the city. It was a time just for The Mission kids, and we filled up all of the six cabins that lined the woods. I loved that place. There were at least ten bunks in each cabin, but we had to walk to get to the toilets and showers. We all ate together, boys and girls, in a large dining hall. I was always one of the first ones in line, especially for dinner as we were all starving from our afternoon swim time in the pool. Crafts were in the morning, and I liked to make stuff, so I always paid attention.

One morning, our camp counselor said we had an important guest. It was a lady dressed like "an Indian." She had a long fringe dress with beads all over, moccasin shoes, and a feather in her hair. She carried a large bag and told us kids we were going to make something very special. Then she told us to sit in a circle, and she sat right in the middle. She told us this story.

Native Americans believe that the night air is filled with dreams, both good and bad. We are going to make something today that captures our dreams. A dream catcher, and when you hang it over or near your bed swinging freely in the air, it catches your dreams as they flow by. The good dreams know how to pass through the dream catcher, slipping through the outer holes and sliding down the soft feathers so gently that many times the sleeper does not know that he or she is dreaming. The bad dreams, not knowing the way, get tangled in the dream catcher and perish with the first light of the new day.

We were enthralled. She then got up and emptied her bag of supplies on the picnic table. There was colored yarn and beads, feathers, tape, needles and thread, and a bunch of round things she called embroidery hoops. She said the Indians used small, bendable branches for their hoops, but this was easier for first-timers.

We all knotted and weaved, braided and knotted some more, and finished our masterpieces by tying small stones and real feathers to the bottom, then loose pieces of yarn. When we were done, she had us kids hold our dream catchers above our heads, and she took a photo. I ran as fast as I could back to my cabin and hung my dream catcher right above my pillow. My prayer had just come true, and I could hardly believe my luck.

You see, Berks County Prison was less than one mile from Camp Joy. If you walked down to the creek on the other side of the woods, you could see the barbed wire fence. At night when we begged for scary stories around the campfire, Mike, our camp counselor, would tell us about this one "lifer" who knew about a gap under the prison fence and would wander our woods at night looking for children to use as hostages. Some campers even thought they saw him once, a crooked old man standing next to a tall, thin boy up on the hill in the moonlight. "He did something so bad that I can't even talk about it," Joe said, leaving us all to imagine the unimaginable.

Even though Mike told us he made the whole thing up before we went to bed, I knew it was entirely possible. There was even a sign near the road that read "PRISON AREA. DO NOT PICK UP HITCHHIKERS." I had bad dreams ever since, so with my new dream catcher, I could finally get some sleep.

Soon our week was up, and we all piled into the bus back to The Mission. When we got back, I decided to tell Tom camp was no fun. He couldn't come, because he was always in punishment, and I didn't want him to feel bad.

CHAPTER 12

Several of the boys came down with boils on their bums. Mrs. Cosenza said it was because they didn't wash properly. No one stayed long in the showers, doing our best to cover our privates, as everyone had to shower together—so I'm not surprised we missed some parts.

But we were all beyond mortified when one day Mrs. Cosenza put her bathing suit on and walked into the boys' shower room! Everyone grew quiet, and I felt my skin tighten. She was coming in with us!

In her arms was a bucket full of rough cleaning pads. She grabbed each of us by the ear, dragged us into the shower stall, and scrubbed our behinds until some boys' bottoms bled. We all went to bed that night with faces as red as our tender behinds.

Like I said, I hated school. I tried to sit in the back and blend in as best I could, never raising my hand—although I knew a lot of the answers.

But one day was different. Everyone seemed to be looking at me—sideways glances and hands hiding whispers—as I made my way to my homeroom. I stopped in the lavatory to make sure something wasn't wrong with my face, hair, or clothes; but I looked the same as every day.

Puzzled and self-conscious, I found my desk and tried to disappear, sliding low in my seat. Our teacher, Mr. Wells, came into the classroom and slowly walked to my desk. "Get your things and come with me please, Robert. And you have done nothing wrong, son."

I did what he said, following him past the principal's office, down a hall to a little lounge area with four large chairs in a circle. He told me to sit down, and he closed the door.

"Robert, first I want to tell you something. Listen to me, son. About a week ago I picked up your brother, Willie, hitchhiking on Bordic Road. I was on my way home from school, and I want to tell you we had a nice visit, and he was very polite and thanked me very much for the ride. Robert, sometimes people can make terrible, terrible mistakes. People can do horrible things to others. People in our own families. People we love. I want you to know that it doesn't mean that you did anything wrong. You understand, son?"

I didn't, but I shook my head *yes.* "Robert, your brother, Willie, is in a lot of trouble. You will hear about it all over the television and newspaper, and it's on the radio too. I'm going to tell you about it, and then I'm going to drive you home to The Children's Home, OK? You can skip school today.

"I'm afraid your brother and a boy named Thomas Lowe kidnapped a young woman last night and drove her to New York City. They are accused of molesting her. Robert, do you know what that means?"

Again I shook my head *yes,* but I wasn't sure I did.

"Son, you will hear the word 'rape.' Do you know what that means?" I pulled my legs up, wrapped my arms around them, and buried my face. That word I knew. "Robert, son, you are a good boy who did nothing wrong. I want you to remember that; promise me? And you are going to have to be brave. People will say mean things. You just come to my office and talk to me, OK? Anytime, about anything." I couldn't answer, still curled up, hands over my ears. "I'm going to drive you back to The Home now. Come on, son. Get your things."

It was all over the television. And the radio. And every newspaper. Every day for months. My big brother, Willie—my hero, my protector, my surrogate father, my everything—was going to prison for twenty-five years.

I just knew they had the wrong boy; Willie would never hurt a girl. I ran to the corner newsstand and saw the headline on every paper, even the *Philadelphia Enquirer* and the *Brooklyn Daily.*

One headline even said, "Berks Abduction Suspect Called Friendless Youth."

When the newsstand man turned his back for a moment, I took a paper and hid it under my shirt, walking away slowly, then running as fast as I could around the corner, out of sight. The paper I had stolen was the *Reading Eagle*, and there on the front page was Willie and Tom Lowe, handcuffed and looking down at the floor.

Under the picture were the words, "Reading Youths Abduct and Assault Teen on a Terror-Filled Ride to Brooklyn, NY."

Two teenage parolees from Reading, PA, were held on $100,000 bail each (that's about $800,000 today!) in Federal Court, Brooklyn, accused of kidnapping an attractive 17-year-old blonde high school student Thursday night and *submitting her to an eight-hour, terror-filled auto ride to Brooklyn during which one of them raped her twice.*

The petite waitress, 5'2" and 110 pounds, was admitted to Kings County Hospital suffering from shock and hysteria after she managed to escape her captors.

The suspects were identified as Thomas Lowe, 18, on probation from an assault and robbery conviction, and Willie Olsen, 17, on parole after doing 20 months of a five-year sentence for the attempted murder of his mother with a baseball bat.

When the waitress left the restaurant to go home at 9:30 p.m. Thursday, Olsen, who is 5'8" and 140 pounds stuck a beer can opener in her back and forced her into a car owned by Lowe's father.

They drove a short distance and then Lowe, who is 6'2" and 180 pounds, forced the victim to remove her clothes and then raped her.

With Olsen doing the driving they took off to New York City, first stopping to buy a bottle of wine which they consumed on the way. Somewhere in New Jersey, Lowe again raped the girl.

They went through the Holland Tunnel and over the Brooklyn Bridge, and at 6 a.m. arrived at Fulton Street, under the bridge. They decided to rob a restaurant at 1 Fulton St. Olsen took the beer can opener and Lowe broke the empty wine bottle to use as weapons.

They told the girl to stay in the car and then crossed the street to enter the restaurant. But the victim, who had been allowed to put her clothes back on after the second rape, jumped out and started to run south on Fulton Street. She signaled frantically to an approaching truck. The two men started to run after her.

The driver of the truck, Joseph Martin, 30, of Lindenhurst, Long Island, slowed down enough so she could jump in the cab beside him, then he sped away. The truck driver spotted a patrol car a few blocks away. The cops sent out an immediate radio alarm, and seconds later another patrol car spotted Lowe getting into the car outside the restaurant, which the pair never got around to robbing. Officers Stanley and Nelson subdued the rugged Lowe after a struggle. They turned him over to other police and continued to cruise about looking for Olsen. They spotted him about seven blocks away. He surrendered without a struggle.

They said Olsen drove the car and fondled the girl, but did not molest her otherwise.

Mr. Cosenza forbade the other kids from talking about it, but they all knew what my brother Willie had done.

I started wetting the bed and having nightmares. "Night terrors," the nurse called them. I tried to hide it, thinking they might take me to the sanitarium with Jeannie if I didn't stop screaming out in the night, the other boys complaining to Mrs. Cosenza. Maybe they would send me for those scalding bath treatments or hook me up to electric wires and shock the crazy out of me like I saw one night on *The Twilight Zone.*

They never did, I kinda got used to the stares and gossip, and people eventually moved on to other news.

But shame never loses its sting.

• • • • •

In the living room of The Mission was an old tapestry on the wall above the sofa. When no one was around, I liked to go in there and look up at it, studying the little village scenes of tiny people tilling the soil and tying up bundles of something. There was a farmer's wife setting out pies to cool on the window of a cute little hut. Threadbare and faded, yet beautiful in its intricacy, I felt that it held a secret. A secret I would never know. How to be a part of something. Something beautiful. Something good.

The Olsens were never a part of something. We were always separate, not quite relaxing into the rhythm of life. We were misfits. We were drunks. We were thieves. And now we were—well, I can't even say that word.

And I wondered if there was something like that hiding inside me too.

CHAPTER 13

One Sunday a month, a family could pick up an orphan and take them home for dinner. Tom would have none of it, but I thought it sounded swell—and maybe the father would show me some cool stuff in his garage.

And I knew something the other kids didn't know. *Francesca's secret.* From our first time here. I remembered what she had whispered to that other girl.

When the visiting Sunday came, Mrs. C woke us early so the ones going to dinner could shower before Bible study. We had to wash our hair and put on the best clothes we had, which weren't good at all but cleaned and ironed. Mrs. C walked down the line, pinching our mouths open to make sure we'd brushed our teeth and threatening us with all kinds of bad if we misbehaved.

When the time came, we kids lined up on the grass next to the side parking lot. Several cars were already waiting, and I began to panic when I didn't see the white Cadillac Francesca had told that girl to watch for. Just when I was getting ready to play sick and go back inside, the white Caddie pulled around to the front. *This was my chance.* I broke the rules and stepped out of line, heart racing, walking quickly over to the Caddie. Thank God Mrs. C hadn't noticed, busy with the girls.

"Hi! My name is Robbie, and I just love your car! Wow, what I wouldn't do for a ride in this car!" Then I gave them the biggest smile I could muster, crossed my fingers, and hoped for the best.

It worked. The man said, "Well now, let's just see if we can make that happen, Robbie!" And off I went, settling into the comfy, soft, red leather back seat.

I was thankful the man and his wife didn't ask me too many questions, and I relaxed a bit when he turned on the car radio. The song "If I Had a Hammer" came on, and the man softly sung along. After a while, we pulled into a long winding drive and up to a very large brick house with white pillars, like those at the bank.

We all went in, and the lady took my jacket and showed me where the bathroom was. Then she went to the kitchen and told me to stay with the man. We went to a large room with a fireplace, and the man asked me to hand him wood from a gold box, and he started a fire. They had a record player inside a cabinet in the big room. I was surprised when the man put on The Beatles—and turned it up pretty loud even! It smelled so good in the house that my mouth kept watering, and I wondered why we weren't eating yet. The lady came back out with a tray holding three fancy glasses. She gave me the one that had a little orange slice stuck on the side and said, "It's a kiddie cocktail, Robert!" I was not a "kiddie" and didn't think I'd like it, but it was delicious.

The lady said their daughter was away at school, and she showed me a picture of a pretty, dark-haired girl in a white dress on the fireplace. A man with long hair in a ponytail came down the stairs. He was nice too and told me he went to law school, but I'd never heard of such a place. He showed me where to wash up before dinner.

The napkins were not paper, and I wasn't sure where they went, but I watched the others. There were too many forks and spoons by my plate, and I must have looked confused, because the lady told me to work "from the outside in." Again, I just watched the others. When she brought low bowls of soup, she told me to scoop away from myself. *They sure have a lot of rules about silverware, I thought.*

Roasted chicken, stuffing, something called Yorkshire pudding. Never in my whole life has anything tasted this good. Not even Mrs. Rosenberg's lunches from the paper box factory, and they were great. I tried hard not to eat fast and thought about putting a few of those rolls into my shirt—but didn't want to take any chances. I needed the man to like me.

By my third helping, the lady reminded me, "I made a lovely dessert, Robert. Don't you want to save a little room for it?" I put my fork down and waited to see what would happen next. The younger man said I was the special guest, so he would clear my dishes away. The lady soon returned with something she called a *black forest cake.* It was all white fluffy frosting, but when she cut me a piece, I could see it was chocolate inside with red cherries. I just knew with the word forest in the name, it would be special. And boy was it.

I knew it was almost time to take me home, and I started to really worry. But then it happened—just like I overheard Francesca say it would. The father took me into that beautiful library, over to his big desk, and opened a drawer. He asked me to open my hand, and in it he placed five shiny new silver dollars. I almost forgot to breathe. It was more money than I had ever seen. I think I heard him saying something about our secret and how it was best not to tell anyone, "lest there are hurt feelings." But I knew that already. I would never, ever, ever tell.

On the ride back to The Mission, all I could think about was where I would hide my precious dollars. I wanted so much to tell George, but Tom had told me never to trust anybody. So on George's day off, I broke into the boiler room and hid my coins between the old file cabinet and the cement wall, wrapped in a piece of old newspaper.

The boiler room had a back hall that led to a storage room of sorts. I started to wander back there to look around, which was totally forbidden—but I just couldn't help myself, so I kept going. It was full of cardboard boxes and old Christmas decorations, a couple of broken bicycles and whatnot.

Then I noticed a large wooden sign that was so weathered it was hard to read. Curious, I wiped it with my sleeve and stepped back to read the faded words. *THE HOME FOR FRIENDLESS CHILDREN, established 1884.* I looked at it for a long time. Wherever this place was, I thought, I would fit in just fine—although the boy with one eye was kind of my friend. I hurried back upstairs before I was missed and Mrs. Cosenza came looking for me.

That night, I dreamed of a big old house where there were no adults, only children wearing long, white night dresses that pooled on the floor around them. Alone in the darkness of locked rooms, their eyes wide, they gazed out from high windows into the night sky.

I realize now that those Sunday dinners with those rich people taught me something important. Something that changed my world view. If I had never overheard Francesca whispering about the family with the white Cadillac, I would not have joined the

Sunday dinner program, gotten my five silver dollars, and most importantly, known *how families could be.* I had thought families like these were only make-believe TV families, like on *Leave It to Beaver.* But now I saw it could be real. No yelling and cussin', just everyone being nice to each other, saying please and thank you all the time, holding hands and saying grace, asking to "please pass this and that," all while pretty music drifts in from the other room. I had never seen anything like it. The man taught me to hold the chair out for the lady, and the lady taught me about different forks and spoons for different foods.

I wanted so much for them to like me that I would try to remember the rules and not to make a mistake.

After a few months, the man told me he liked to pick up a new child every few months or so to keep things fair, but said he was *very glad he got to meet me.*

That was the last time I got to see the man who gave me the silver dollars, and the lady who cooked delicious dinners and said I was a delightful boy. I continued the Sunday orphan dinners for a few more months, visiting different families, but it was never the same. One day I just stopped going, instead staying back to play basketball with Tom.

CHAPTER 14

Every year *The Times* newspaper sponsored the Reading City Marbles Tournament. This was a big deal. The winner got a $10 gift certificate to the Hobby Store, their picture in the newspaper, and a congratulations letter from the superintendent of schools, Mr. Ralph Geigle.

The only part of that I cared about was the $10 from the Hobby Store. Heck, that money along with my five silver dollars hiding in the boiler room would allow me to buy all the car model kits I longed for, along with everything I needed for my rocket and launch pad. I *had* to win.

The problem was, I didn't have any marbles. No one in The Mission had marbles, ever since the marble fight the last Christmas that had chipped a girl's front tooth.

I had a thought. I had just started sixth grade at Riverside Grade School, so I decided to ask around and try to find a bag-full. I had no luck, until I smuggled my precious slingshot into school, showing it to some kids on the playground. It was painful to give it up. It was beautiful and my only defense in The Mission—although the mean kids had already left me alone for fear of Tom.

It worked. Three kids brought bags of marbles the next day. I traded for the biggest bag so I could share them with Tom.

I could only practice at recess on the playground at school, but I caught on quickly and felt confident enough to sign up. I won. Then I won the District Three Championship the following week.

Mrs. Cosenza insisted I wear a jacket and tie from the clothing donation room, and she helped me comb my hair to the side. It was the first time she was ever nice to me. A photographer from *The Times* took my picture in the big room where we put the tree at Christmas time.

The headline above my picture read, "BOB IS KING OF MIBS RING," It was nice, but I guess no one told them my name is Rob. It went on:

Mibster Bobby Olsen, the marble tournament champ at Riverside Grade School, this Thursday afternoon defended his title at the District Three Championship. But the road to victory was not smooth. The competition was keen and tough. The round robin playoff—where each mibster plays the others in a specified number of games—ended in a three-way tie. The result was another round robin among the three. It was getting dark and the lights were put on in the fieldhouse when Bobby, Debra Dingle, a sixth grader at Glenside, and third grader Albert Bonetti from Charles F. Foos Grade School finished shooting. Bobby took the title by a slim margin, winning four games of the six each rolled. Close behind, with three victories, was Albert, a serious lad who concentrated before every shot.

I even received a card in a small white envelope with a gold seal. It read:

May 25, 1967

Dear Bobby,

Congratulations on your tremendous performance in the marbles tournament.

I am,

Very respectfully yours,

Ralph Geigle

Superintendent of Schools

Reading, Pa.

Mrs. Cosenza took my $10 gift certificate and "put it away for safekeeping," she said. I told her I wanted to keep it with me, but soon gave up and handed it over. There was no arguing with Mrs. C.

Tom was a bit jealous, I think, and the very next year he entered the competition too. I'd see him in the back of the basketball court on Saturdays, practicing his shots inside a chalk circle he would draw—and then erasing the marks quickly if the playground matron came around. He got pretty good at marbles, and we both won our schools' championships. This time it was Tom's picture in the paper.

But he wasn't happy at all. In fact, he was angry.

The headline read "ADD AN OLSEN TO FINALS TODAY!" Under Tom's picture, it read:

An Olsen did it again. This time it was Tom who won a school championship in the Times-sponsored City Marbles Tournament. On Tuesday afternoon, Bobby Olsen rolled his way to the Northwest Junior High School title. And on Wednesday afternoon, brother Tom earned the Riverside Grade School laurels in Baer Park Field House by defeating schoolmates in a best-out-of-five contest.

You see, here is the problem. Tom was two years older than me, but he had failed two grades, so he was a year behind me in school. I had moved on to junior high, while he was still in grade school. Now everyone else who read the paper knew it too. Tom would carry that chip on his shoulder the rest of his life, and it would cost him dearly.

Life carried on at The Mission, kids coming and going. Almost three years passed, then just like the last time, one day we were going home.

THE ORPHANAGE

CORNERSTONE

CHAPTER 15

Mom had moved out of the trailer and was living in a rowhome apartment back in our old neighborhood, a few blocks from Arlene and Ray's. I was super happy to find a Hobby Store on our block—and a hardware store too! But my happiness disappeared shortly after we got home, when I realized that Mom was still with Jack. I started to wish she hadn't picked us up, even though she promised he was "different now." I knew better.

For a while, he seemed to make an effort with Tom and me, even taking us along with him in his pickup once to help load some roofing shingles. But it didn't last. He and Mom were soon fighting again, mostly after a night at the old bar.

Our new landlord was a super nice man named Mr. Moretti. When Mom picked us up from The Mission, he was waiting in the street to welcome us home. Mom said he owned several rentals on Spruce Street, and that he was an Alderman for the city, whatever that meant. He seemed to know everyone, and I even heard some people call him "your honor." And he always waved to me when he drove by in his silver Eldorado, one time stopping to buy us kids Dreamsicles from the ice cream truck.

Yep, I liked him a lot. Especially because he did not like Jack. At all.

One night I got home late from a friend's house to find Mr. Moretti's Eldorado and a police car in front of our house. I ran past them both and found Mom in a kitchen chair holding a dishcloth over her bloody mouth. Jack had hit Mom so hard he knocked her two front teeth lose, and one was hanging lose backward over her gums. Jack was nowhere to be found, and Mr. Moretti asked me to wait outside for a few minutes.

After a while, Mr. Moretti came out holding mom's arm. "I'm taking your mother to the hospital, and I want you to lock the door and not answer for anyone," he instructed. About midnight, I heard Mom come home and go right to her room, locking the door behind her.

No one ever saw Jack again. There was even a rumor around the neighborhood that there had been an "airing" and that Jack was at the bottom of the Schuylkill River, his feet encased in a cement bock—Mr. Moretti being Italian and all. One day I borrowed a neighbor's bike and rode clear to the river. I rode up and down the riverbank, looking for signs of anything suspicious or out of place. But it just looked like it always did, so I rode home, feeling a bit guilty that I hoped he was fish food down there at the bottom.

Mom moped around for weeks, rarely saying a word to Tom and me when she got home from her job at the laundromat. She looked different with those teeth missing and a few weeks later had them all pulled. "I'm not messing with the dentist anymore!" she announced when she returned home looking like one of those dried-apple dolls at the Hobby Store. About a month later, she got a pair of ill-fitting dentures that she complained about for years.

Most evenings she would change clothes and walk to a new bar, three blocks over from Arlene and Ray's. I knew this, because I followed her once.

She probably got tired of all the talk about Jack and just wanted to be left alone, I thought. But I was wrong about that.

One day she came home carrying a bag from Pomerey's Department Store. She reached in and pulled out a green dress with some tickets hanging from the sleeve. "To match my eyes," she laughed, twirling as she held it up for approval.

"It's pretty, Mom," I said, happy to see my mother smiling.

"I've got a date," she said, and went in to take a bath.

Turns out our landlord, Mr. Moretti, had arranged for Mom to meet another tenant of his, a widower named Charlie Caruso. Charlie was Italian like Mr. Moretti, and Mom said the wops always helped their own.

I was worried about the whole thing. We didn't need another man coming around. But when he showed up to pick up Mom for the date, I liked him right away. He was a slight man with brown hair and a kind face. His voice was so soft. I had to lean in to hear him, and when I did, I noticed his hands were shaking. I liked the way he helped Mom put on her coat, just like my Sunday dinner man had done with his wife. And he even said goodbye to me.

From the window, I watched Charlie take Mom's arm and help her across the street to the bus stop where they caught the six o' clock for an Italian restaurant across town.

The next Saturday night, Mom made "spaghettis" and invited Charlie to dinner. He hardly said one word but cleaned his plate and even had seconds.

The next Saturday, they were married at the Reading courthouse.

• • • • •

Charlie left his apartment and moved in with us on Spruce Street. It was just me, Mom, and Charlie. Tom had been arrested for selling pot and was back in juvie, and of course nobody talked about where Jeannie was.

Charlie worked at Oritskys Clothing Factory. There are lots of clothing factories in Reading. In fact, buses full of New York City shoppers fill the factory parking lots the week after Thanksgiving for their annual overstock and "seconds" sale. All the brand names are here, according to mom. "Those rich people from New York buy the seconds, and then go to their fancy parties fooling everybody but me!" She liked to say. Charlie told me he had been working there twenty-two years, pressing men's slacks on a giant steam press. He said Oritskys made fine men's suits for some brothers named Brooks, and that they had a fancy men's clothing store on Madison Avenue in New York City. Charlie got Mom a job there too, running a sewing machine.

Charlie never talked, but when he did it was to tell Mom how *delicious* dinner was or to tell me how smart I was. He once told me that his father was a mean man who never taught him anything and made him drop out of school in sixth grade. He was sorry about that and wished he knew more stuff, he said.

With both Mom and Charlie working at Oritskys, we always had food, and that Christmas, I got the train I had been aching for from the window of the Hobby Shop. With my paper route money, I could buy some tracks and model buildings too. It was the happiest I had ever felt—ever, ever, ever. Even better than having five silver dollars.

• • • • •

It was 1969, and it seemed like the whole world was gaga crazy mad about the Apollo Space Mission. But maybe no one more than me. I was glued to the evening news most nights, along with Charlie. Mom didn't seem to care too much – teasing us from the kitchen. I decided right then and there to build a rocket that would go higher than all my previous rockets I had fired from the old mill parking lot. Yep, this one would be different. I'm fourteen years old and I'm aiming for the moon.

Now I realized none of the model rocket kits at the hobby store had rocket bodies long enough for my crazy idea. I had a thought. I asked mom to bring me home some cardboard tubes from Oritskys, the kind that are in the middle of a long roll of fabric. Two days later she came through for me, bringing home a six foot long one!

That will be an amazing rocket length and allow me to make a multiple stage rocket, just like NASA.

Now the engines. Rocket engines are made by the Estes Company, and you can buy them at any hobby store, five for a dollar. They are about four inches long and 3/4" diameter. Over simplified, there are 2 types of engines. Lower stage engines designed to burn through their entire thrust until their propellants are exhausted, and then ignite the engine above it without any delay whatsoever. Upper stage engines thrust for the same period, pausing for 6 seconds before backfiring to push out the next stage and so on, and finally the parachute and payload.

My crazy design was 4 stages, and should fly 5000 feet up, *if I'm lucky.*

My best friend Dennis begged me to let him put his pet mouse Mr. Pips in the payload. Now I wasn't sure about this. After my sad turtle incident, I swore I would never hurt an animal ever again. But Dennis had sent him up before, in a smaller model rocket from the hobby store, and he was just fine, only a little dizzy, so I agreed.

I built balsa wood fins to act like the feathers on an arrow, and a launch pad, but bought the other rocket parts, including the little parachute and payload compartment, and all the engines I needed.

I decided to name my rocket Armstrong. I had just built a model of the X-15, a hypersonic rocket powered aircraft built by the US Air Force that broke all speed and altitude records in 1967, reaching a speed of 4,534 miles an hour, and a height of 67 miles. Neil Armstrong was one of the few pilots who flew the X-15, and now on the news I found out he was going to the moon! I just had to name my rocket after him.

The plan was made.

Rocket ignition and liftoff from launch pad.

High thrust and acceleration for flight.

Stage one burns

Stage 2 burns

Stage 3 burns

Stage 4 burns

Rocket streaks skyward to peak altitude.

Rocket reaches peak altitude and ejection charge activates recovery system.

Recovery parachute is deployed.

Mr. Pips returns safely to earth. Maybe.

We set a date and word spread. When the big day came the weather was perfect. All we had to do was pray that our six feet of fabric tubing wasn't too heavy, that our fins stayed on, and most importantly, that our rocket didn't decide to tilt sideways off course and ruin everything and start chasing everyone on the ground.

My friend Joe came over early to help carry our rocket to the abandoned Textile Chemical Company parking lot. When we got there a crowd of kids had already began to gather, a jumble of bikes dropped under the only tree near the deserted parking lot.

We went thru the prelaunch checklist and made sure the parachute was loaded correctly. Everyone was getting crazy excited. Dennis carried over Mr. Pips and we all wished him luck, some with tears in their eyes. Mr. Pips was the bravest dude we ever knew. We carefully slid Mr. Pips into the top of the rocket, secured the nose, and then placed the rocket on the Launchpad. I hooked up the wires and we all retreated to our launch positions.

10….. 9……..8……..7……..6……..5…….4……3……2…….1… Ignition ! ! ! !

Now understand that model rockets accelerate at the speed of light. One second it's there, and the next second it is five hundred feet up in the sky, unlike the Apollo missions where the rockets move upward in what seems like slow motion.

BLASTOFF ! Smoke was everywhere, sliding along the ground towards us and curling up around the launch pad. We couldn't see the rocket for a couple seconds, just like the launch of the Apollo missions on TV. This was amazing and worrisome at the same time. It didn't blast off like the other rockets we had launched. I had been concerned about this due to all the extra weight but this was extreme. It was moving in slow motion as everyone started hooting and hollering as it struggled to lift. I was the only one that really knew that this wasn't all great. It needed to move faster to reach altitude.

Thankfully it started speeding up, and then dropped the bottom engine along with the stage one fins. Now it started to soar, moving faster and faster and still going straight up while the gang screamed with joy. Second stage finished, stage three ignited, and still soaring! I'm recalculating. *At this rate I'm not gonna make it to the moon.*

Stage 4 burned out at about 1000 feet. Not quite the 5000 foot target, and the most critical moment was upon us. There is a six second delay before that engine backfires to eject the parachute so Mr. Pips can begin his journey back to earth. Everyone held their breath, the Catholic boys making the sign of the cross.

All of the rocket guys knew that sometimes the parachute doesn't eject like it is supposed to. All eyes gazed at the sky, counting what seemed like the longest six seconds ever. The rocket was finishing its arc as it began to run out of speed. Just as I was getting scared something was wrong, there was a big black puff of smoke. We all knew what that meant, and everyone starting jumping up and down with tears in our eyes. Mr. Pips is coming home.

The wind carried the parachute about 100 yards further south than I had calculated. Oh oh. As we all ran towards the landing area, the rocket and payload touched down with what seemed to be a fairly hard impact. Since I was the fastest runner, I was there first. I waited for Dennis to catch up because I knew he would want to know if Mr. Pips made it. And he would want to be there if the news wasn't so good. Finally Dennis caught up, followed by the rest of the boys. We all gathered around.

The moment is here. The moment that finalized our failed mission to the moon. We all held our breath as we opened the capsule. Ever so slowly I pried off the nose cone and peaked in. Two little dark eyes met mine.

I poured Mr. Pips gently into Dennis's waiting hands. He didn't move. Dennis blew a gentle breath on Mr. Pips and we all prayed. All of a sudden Mr. Pips moved, and then Dennis placed him tenderly him on the ground. He stood up and started walking around all dizzy-like! Everyone started cheering and jumping up and down with relief. Mr. Pips was A-OK, and Armstrong made it back too!

• • • • •

One day, I borrowed a bike and rode to the paper box factory behind Arlene and Ray's. The truck I had ridden in to make deliveries while working there was backed up to the door. I stayed behind the neighbor's garage across the street, out of sight but near enough to hear both machines running. *A big order.* They must need help. I started slowly walking over, but turned around and stayed hidden, my insides beginning to ache. I wondered if they ever thought about me. But I was fifteen now, and, well, Mom said nobody wants teenagers. I watched for a long time, then I rode home and never went back again.

I got a summer job washing dishes at the Woodward Cafe around the corner and picked up a second early paper route near our neighborhood. By the end of the summer, I had saved enough for more train track for the station I had built in our basement—and a used bicycle, which made my paper deliveries a lot shorter for sure. Tom was still in juvie, so I didn't have to worry about him taking it; but I still carried it up to my room every night for safekeeping.

I started Reading High School in the fall. I tried to keep to myself, hoping no one knew I ever had lived in The Mission. I did everything to try to hide it. The few high school friends I had still didn't know, or if they did, they were quiet about it.

But everyone knew about Willie. I was *the kid whose brother was in prison.*

*E*ven though I kept a low profile, I just couldn't help myself and one day joined the Camera Club. I had almost saved enough to buy the Pentax XM Camera I had my eye on. Back in The Mission, one of the boys got a camera and film for Christmas—from an uncle, he had said—and let me shoot a few pictures on the playground. I had wanted one ever since. I just needed to save ten more dollars.

And just like that, it almost fell into my pocket.

• • • • •

A boy named Henry and his father worked at the Woodward Cafe with me. Henry cleared tables, and his dad was a waiter, driving in thirty minutes from Robesonia every afternoon. It never made sense to me, the gas money and all, but they never missed a day of work.

One day Henry came over to my dishwashing station and whispered, "Hey Robbie, I need to talk to you about something—in PRIVATE." So on our ten-minute break, I met him outside the back door. He lit a ciggie, leaned into me, and asked, "How would you like to make an easy ten bucks?" My heart quickened, as this was the exact amount I was short for the Pentax camera I wanted.

All I had to do, he said, was call the phone number he had written down at 7:00 a.m. tomorrow morning and tell whoever answered that I had planted a bomb in the lockers—and then hang up. It sounded pretty simple, although I knew it was wrong.

I thought about that cool Pentax and agreed. They would never find me. Henry attended Conrad Weiser High School in Robesonia, twenty miles away from my school. They would never suspect a kid from Reading High.

Still, I woke with an uneasy feeling, a foreboding if you will. I called anyway, from a phone booth on the corner of Chestnut and Elm. I said exactly what Henry said to say. I lowered my voice as best I could, and blurted out "I PUT A BOMB IN THE LOCKER ROOM!" I hung up quickly, stepped out of the phone booth, and headed to school—dreaming of my new Pentax.

It was all over the papers and even on TV. I tried to act normal and went to work after school like always. Henry and his dad were already there, and Henry slipped me my ten bucks as he was unloading a cart of dirty dishes to my station. All was well for a few days, and I started to relax—until on the fourth day, I returned home to a police car in front of our house.

Turns out Henry had bragged to some kids that he was behind the whole thing, and when someone talked, he spilled the beans. I was arrested, handcuffed, and taken downtown. I was scared out of my freaking mind and cried like a baby in the detective's office, until Mom and Charlie showed up and calmed me down. Jack would have beat the crap out of me, but Charlie kept rubbing my back as I sat forward with my face buried in my hands. It seemed like we were there for hours; then all of a sudden, I was allowed to go home.

I was expelled from school, and my court date was set. The day before I was to stand before the magistrate—and surely be sent to juvie—Mom got a phone call, and someone told her to take me to the probation officer instead.

Turns out Charlie had called Joe Moretti and asked for help as soon as they heard what happened. I don't know what Mr. Moretti told the magistrate, but Mom was almost giddy as she explained to me that "all the charges have been dropped, Robbie!" Joe Moretti sure was "somebody" in this Mafia town. "All you have to do is help clean the school on Saturdays for three months", mom told me, "and you can go back to school, but you are not to ever speak of it again." And you can bet I never did.

While I had a near-miss with the law, Mom's life was getting more put together. She seemed to take an interest in what I was doing for the first time ever, and even took the time to look at my rocket design sketchbook. She even got a driver's license! Charlie had never learned and didn't want to try driving, but Mom was super proud as she showed me her official card with her picture on it. The neighbor lady had taught her, so Mom marched right over to her house—and they all celebrated with something called Manhattans on her front porch.

Soon, Mom was the proud owner of a green Plymouth convertible, complete with a little payment book she kept in a bowl on the side table.

LEFT: ROCKET LAUNCHING.

BELOW: FAVORITE LAUNCH SITE.

CHAPTER 16

I began to lose interest in my basement train station and started thinking how cool it would be to blow the whole thing up. I kept thinking about *The Adams Family* episode where Lurch brings the school superintendent into the dining room to find Gomez running his elaborate train set on a massive dining room table. He has his hands on both handles of the little black control box, shoulders hunched up, elbows out, ready to push down.

"Ahhh…just in time," he tells the superintendent. "Want to blow her up?"

"What?!" shouts the man. "You will destroy the whole thing!"

"Well," laughs Gomez, "why else would a grown man play with a train set?!" BOOM!

Executing my idea would take a lot of careful planning, some mathematical calculations on explosives, a little luck, and an afternoon when I was home while Mom and Charlie were not. Also, I had no money, so my explosive material would have to come from stuff I already had or could find at the junkyard.

Wire—check.

Firecrackers—check.

M 80—check.

Generator—check.

Igniter box—check.

I spent months preparing. I had two engines, so I decided it would be way-cool to have a second track going in the opposite direction at the same time, with explosives on each. That way, I could time the explosions one after the other, in close succession for maximum impact.

I decided to build a large Balsa-wood bridge for the grand finale. Balsa is light and brittle, so the parts would really fly. I used my rocket technology to wire the firecrackers and carefully opened the M80 to remove just the right amount of material to do the job, without blowing up the house. I had three coal cars that I filled with real coal, crushed to a fine powder, that I had collected down at the railroad tracks. They would be perfect little auxiliary bombs. I placed the post office, bank, and grocery next to the coal cars, so they would blow too. *Holy crap, this is going to rock!*

I grabbed the firecrackers, took out the fuses, replaced them with rocket igniters, and wired them to my sequential electric generator. I glued the firecrackers to the bottom of the bridge for maximum effect. Then I carefully pried open the M80 and sprinkled the powder along the main girder, with a little sprinkled on the seismic isolators I had designed out of toilet paper tubes. Then I ran the wire to my little control station behind the plexiglass shield I had found at the junkyard. Can't be too careful.

Next Sunday, Mom and Charlie were taking the bus to visit Aunt Tilly in New Jersey, and after some begging, I convinced them to let me stay home.

Now, the boys. I hopped on my bike and drove up and down Spruce Street, passing the word, making everyone swear a pledge of secrecy—especially Tom O'Hare whose dad was a cop.

Sunday couldn't come soon enough. I tried to act normal and prayed no one went downstairs to the basement. I had covered the track with an old sheet, just in case, and made myself scarce. I thought I looked guilty of *something.*

I woke up with second thoughts. What if the M80 is too much? What if it is a dud? What if no one comes? Geez, of course they will come! And I had made such careful calculations.

Mom and Charlie finally left for the bus station, so I flew downstairs to make final preparations, dreaming of my new status that would surely follow.

The kids started showing up—even Joe Talerico, who was five years older but had heard and didn't want to miss out. The train platform was plywood on sawhorses, taking up most of the basement's back room. There was only about a foot of space around the whole thing, with a small square cutout in the back where I would stand as conductor.

I entered the room by crawling under the platform to my little station. My rule was the boys had to stay outside the room, but could watch from the doorway. Starting at the bottom of the door, all their heads lined up like a totem pole, one on top of the other, with Joe Talerico's head at the top. Bodies safely behind the cinder-block wall. I had started both trains up before the guys got there. My little city was ready for the disaster that would soon befall.

I returned to my station, safe behind the plexiglass shield. My heart was pounding as I placed both hands on the little detonator box and pushed down hard.

BOOM!!! The bank blew to smithereens. *Damn! I think the coal car idea was a mistake.*

BOOM!!! The post office hit the ceiling hard, but miraculously stayed in one piece.

BOOM!!! The grocery store was pretty cool, although it shot toward the boys and could have taken an eye out had they not ducked. *Yep, the coal was a disaster!* Black soot was freaking everywhere. But the explosions went off in perfect order, with the grand finale—the balsa wood bridge next. A spine-chilling fear surged in my chest. Too late, no stopping now.

BOOM! BOOM! BOOM! Black smoke, train parts, balsa wood, and coal flew everywhere!!!

Everybody ran like hell. A few minutes later, I heard a pounding on the front door. I hid. Whoever it was must have left, but I heard the phone ringing upstairs. Then quiet. In my neighborhood, you didn't ask too many questions. No one wanted to know too much in case the cops came around looking for information, and you might be labeled a snitch.

I opened the windows, threw out all the burned parts and my stinky clothes, and scrubbed the ceiling with Mr. Clean. Then I gave up on the rest, took a bath, got under the covers, and prayed. I must have fallen asleep, as I woke to Charlie sitting on the bed.

"Tell me what happened, Robbie. And I want the truth." I was never so grateful that Charlie was a kind and gentle man. I told him everything. I'm sure it was like Catholic confession that my Italian friends dreaded. But it felt kinda good to tell Charlie, instead of holding my secret crime inside. He listened carefully to the whole story, then said, "Robbie, you are lucky the police didn't come and take you to juvie with Tom. Now, don't ever do anything like that again, and clean the basement good in the morning while we are at work. Be thankful your mom was too tired to notice anything. Good night, son."

And life returned to normal on Spruce Street.

"Be weird. Be random. Be who you are."

—Unknown

CHAPTER 17

One day, Mom announced that we were all going on a trip to Florida so her folks could meet Charlie. It was just the three of us. I felt bad Tom couldn't join us, but he had gotten in trouble again. Mom refused to let him come home, so back to The Mission he went for the third time.

It took us three days by bus to get to my grandparents' house on Commercial Boulevard in Fort Lauderdale. They picked us up from the bus station in a 1965 pale-blue Chevy Nova with a stick shift on the column. My grandmother, Helen, was cold and distant, always a little loopy from her daily dose of phenobarbital, according to Mom. But my grandfather, William, seemed kind.

I didn't know them at all. They had never showed any interest in us—or in their only daughter, for that matter.

When I was in The Mission, I used to daydream that my grandparents would show up one day and take me away to Florida with them, where I would become a world-class surfer; but that never happened.

One day on our visit, my grandfather surprised us with a car trip down to a place called Key West. We were all packed into the Chevy like sardines and held our breath every time a car passed us on the narrow and harrowing Seven Mile Bridge. Grandpa said the bridge was originally a railroad bridge, and people even called it "the eighth wonder of the world," because "no one thought you could build a bridge over seven miles of open water and a soft bottom in such a harsh tropical climate," he explained.

It was the first time in my life that I stayed in a motel. It was called The Southernmost. I guess because it was the southernmost place in the country, according to Grandpa. It was also the first time I ate in a restaurant besides my birthday lunch at Woolworths. We took a little train tour one day, but otherwise I never got out of the pool.

On either side of the motel were the most magnificent mansions I had ever seen, even on TV. My favorite was a huge Victorian with turrets and a parapet, although I certainly didn't know those terms at the time. I just called them the "castles next door." I liked to walk over by the homes in the cool evenings when I was waterlogged from swimming all day. I'd stand by the street, outside the manicured boxwood hedge, and imagine my life in that house.

My bedroom would be in that high turret part with that pretty iron balcony. My bed would be next to that little window, where I would study the stars and listen to the sea. I would have many friends, because I would be rich, and we would swim and have ice cream on the lawn under that striped awning.

Soon, it was time to catch the bus back home. I never saw or talked to my grandparents again.

CHAPTER 18

My brother, Tom—two years older than me—spent his entire childhood in and out of juvie. That is, when he wasn't in The Mission. No one, and I mean *no one messed with* Tom. Which meant that when Tom was around, no one messed with me. This was pretty great, seeing that I had thick glasses and bad hair, and well, you know how kids are.

I loved Tom. Since Willie went to prison when I was twelve, Tom was everything to me. I had no dad, a retarded sister far away in a sanitarium, another sister I'd never met, and a drunk mother who kept losing custody of us.

I have to admit that I wasn't all that upset when social services would show up with papers and a police car to take me and Tom away for a few days. As long as I was with Tom, I was safe.

But all that changed when Tom up and ran away from The Mission and joined the Air Force at seventeen.

Tom hated authority of any kind—always had. In fact, he lost any job he ever had within a few days, usually for mouthing off to his superiors. So no one was surprised that in less than one year of serving, Tom was charged with insubordination and thrown in the brig.

Although none of us knew where our father was, we knew he had a half-brother named Jack who worked for the government in DC. We had heard all kinds of rumors as kids that he was a secret agent, traveling the world incognito. Well Tom, being Tom, tried to find Uncle Jack while he was in confinement. And damn if he didn't, complete with a phone number. Jack was not a secret agent, but he was way up high in the US Maps Department. Yep, they have one. Tom called Uncle Jack and begged him to write a letter on his behalf to the Air Force explaining Tom's horrendous and abusive childhood, and its effect on Tom's behavior concerning authority figures.

It worked. Tom was out of the brig after two years and on his way home with only a dishonorable discharge. Then he disappeared for years.

CHAPTER 19

On June 22, 1972, my life changed forever. Two weeks after I graduated high school, an epic storm hit Reading, Pennsylvania. It developed as a tropical depression in the Caribbean, progressed into a storm the next day as it traveled north, then strengthened into Hurricane Agnes by the time it reached us.

The most significant damage by far occurred in Pennsylvania, mostly due to intense flooding. When Agnes hit, they were still constructing the Blue Marsh Dam, which was being built to try to prevent flooding of this magnitude. The water quickly reached the heart of the city where we lived. The Schuylkill River, a few blocks away, reached a record height of 31.5 feet, a whopping 15 feet above flood stage! We woke to the sound of sirens and could hardly make out the public announcement blaring from down the street. Mom, Charlie, and I, half asleep, opened the basement door to a floating mess all the way up to the third step, and rising fast. The police cars could not make it down the street, so the policemen walked in thigh-high water, ordering everyone to evacuate to the high school immediately. "Leave everything behind," was the order. "Leave *NOW.*"

I tore upstairs and put what was left of my train set on my tall dresser, along with my albums and turntable. I almost put my camera up there too, but at the last second tucked it into my jacket's high inside pocket; that camera was my most valuable possession, after all. We were going to have to walk through water, and I was taking no chances. Mom was yelling for me, so I took one last look around and ran downstairs. By the time we left the house, the water was up to our front porch. We waded waist deep in the rain through the river that used to be Spruce Street. Charlie was quietly crying, but Mom—a tough old bird—had a look of defiance as we made our way up the street to higher ground at the high school.

We were given dry clothes from the Red Cross lady and assigned three cots near the middle of the gymnasium. Agnes was pounding Pennsylvania. There was a small TV mounted high on the wall and a news report from Philly showed the utter devastation. We listened as we laid on our cots, clutching the thin blankets they gave us, each in our own thoughts, each realizing nothing would ever be the same. Forty-eight people dead, 68,000 homes destroyed, 220,000 people homeless. *And it's still raining.*

President Nixon, deep in the throes of Watergate, took time to fly by helicopter over our city, declaring a national disaster.

Pennsylvania's Governor Milton Sharp called the storm "Hurricane Agony."

"Her name was Agnes. She wore anything but paint and powder. Instead of a smile, she carried a scepter wrought by wind and rain. Her touch was disaster," wrote reporter Cal Turner of The Evening News.

One newspaper headline simply read, "BATTERED, LASHED, FLOODED, and PARALYZED!"

Four days after the flood my girlfriend, Loni, told me she was pregnant.

• • • • •

We were allowed to go home for a short visit, only to see what was left of our homes. There was an official police order that no one could move back in. Our city was declared a disaster zone and our street condemned. Our world was a brown mess. Mud covered every possible surface—every house, every street, every car, every yard. We walked home in total shock, only to find that thieves had robbed us. My trains, albums, and all my stuff had disappeared, along with anything of value in our home. There was no such thing as insurance in our world, and Charlie was so sad and hopeless, that they just walked away from it all—never returning to the house ever again. They called my mom's aunt, Tilly, in Saddlebrook; bought two bus tickets to New Jersey; and were gone the next day.

They wanted me to come too, but I couldn't bring myself to desert Loni. *Shit, shit, shit. I didn't want a baby. I didn't want a wife. I wanted a better life than I had known.*

I had to find a place to sleep, and I had to find a job. I was seventeen.

I ended up crashing at Loni's house, on the sofa. She still hadn't told her mom. I kept hoping and praying the pregnancy would go away, that it was all a bad dream—but it wasn't. I told Loni I didn't love her, but deep in my heart I knew I would never do what my father did, so I stayed.

We had a church wedding. I asked Dave Jett who was the cook at the Woodward Cafe to be my best man. He had taken me under his wing when I was the dishwasher there in eleventh grade. I even named my son David after him when he was born one month later.

• • • • •

The Reading clothing factories opened back up, so Mom and Charlie came home to their old jobs at Oritskys Clothing Factory, getting temporary housing at the YMCA on Washington Street. Mom returned to her sewing machine, and Charlie to his giant steamer press.

So many people never returned to work after the flood, so I was hired easily into a position at the factory. I was a "spreader." Eight hours a day, I spread large rolls of fabric several layers thick across a table, lining them up perfectly. Then the "cutter" person would do their thing, I'd move the fabric to another table, and start the whole process over again.

I hated it. I was bored out of my mind with the repetition, but the money wasn't bad. One day I was pretty tired as David had been up all night with a fever. I forgot to remove my hand from my spreader table in time, and got "nicked" by the machine. Management sent me to first aid to address my hand. The nurse had me roll up my sleeve, and then suddenly stopped what she was doing, looked at me intensely, and asked "Are you a cutter?" I just stared at her and blinked a few times....... "A what?" I asked. "A cutter!" She responded. "Someone who cuts themselves when depressed." "Huh? I blinked a couple more times. "Hell no!" I answered a bit too loudly. "I used to climb a lot of trees and build stuff. I like junk yards. I'm always getting cut. What's the big deal?" We both looked down at my forearm. Geez, I guess she was right. It did look like a "big deal." My arms were covered with nicks and scars ranging from tiny to two inches long. Tiny burn marks too - thanks to my rocket and bomb-making days.

• • • • •

I owned a house before I owned a car. One day out of the blue, Mom called Aunt Tilly. She and her husband, Ed, owned the popular Ed's Tavern in Saddlebrook, New Jersey. She asked Tilly to loan me $1,000 for a down payment on a $10,000 two-unit row home on Weiser Street in Reading. Loni, David, and I would take the larger, two-bedroom upper unit—with Mom and Charlie renting the downstairs unit from me.

I bought a used TV so Loni and I could watch our favorite TV show, *Kung Fu*. I admired Shaolin monk and martial arts expert, Caine, as he wandered the Old West defending the helpless and defeating the bad guys with amazing moves, all while searching for his half-brother and evading the Chinese sent to kill him. I loved it so much that I signed up for karate classes at The George Dillman Karate Institute. And as crazy as life was, I had no idea who I would meet while training there.

George Dillman was a professional boxer for three years and the only person known to have trained with both Bruce Lee and Muhammad Ali. I guess it was just luck that he had chosen the Reading area to set up shop. The classes were demanding, and I trained hard and moved up quickly with my belts. My least favorite part of class was the actual sparring. I preferred to practice the flowing *katas* Caine had mastered on *Kung Fu*. It was rare to find George sparring with the students, as he was usually traveling and giving seminars around the world. But one day, he was there and came into my class. No one wanted to spar with him, but I guess my Olsen roots came out, and I stood up. He knocked me on my ass within two minutes.

One day, a new student joined us. Our sensei said she was a special guest and to treat her with great respect. She smiled warmly and sat down with the rest of us. When her turn came, she had the most graceful kata I had ever seen, but she did not spar with the rest of us, sitting perfectly still as she watched us without emotion. I noticed the students sneaking glances at her, and some were outright staring. She was pretty, and I wondered what high school she had gone to. In the locker room after class, I was stunned to find out she was Muhammad Ali's wife, Khalilah, who had married him at seventeen.

I was having trouble with my 360 Crescent, a karate move where the practitioner jumps into the air and executes a 360 turn while keeping the body perpendicular to the ground. I decided to splurge and treat myself to a private lesson. My sensei offered a discount if one other student would join in on a private. You can imagine my surprise when Khalilah Ali walked in to join me. She was acting as my "other student"! I was so starstruck and nervous, I made little progress with my 360 and hardly defended myself when we sparred. After a few weeks she never came again, and someone said it was because she was going to have a baby.

Although I never saw him, it was rumored that Ali himself would visit the school after-hours to train with George. You see, The Champ had left his training camp in Miami and bought six acres in Deer Lake, just outside of Reading. He loved the secluded, wooded property just ninety miles from Philly and built a training camp there—sometimes laboring with the help, hauling lumber with the best of them.

While the camp's thirteen buildings were being constructed, Ali trained with his friend, Dillman, at the very school I attended in Reading. Of course we never saw Ali, since the school closed to us whenever he showed up.

It was rumored he resided in a trailer on his property and was often spotted riding his horse through the meadows and forest that were his refuge. A small, white mosque was built on the property where he would pray five times a day, and it is said that there were eighteen huge boulders scattered around the camp, all painted by Ali's father. On them were the names of famous boxers, including one for Ali. I heard that Ali's favorite rock was reportedly the one that honored Sonny Liston, the fighter he beat in 1964 to take the heavyweight title.

Ali eventually sold the training camp to Dillman in the 1990s. He would occasionally return to the remote camp he had worked so hard to build—the last visit being in 2001. With the ailing champ suffering from Parkinson's disease, the best he could do was peer at his beloved camp through a limousine window.

• • • • •

As I said, Caine from *Kung Fu* was my hero, and I tried to emulate his behavior—hoping it would bring me the peace I so longed for. Turns out I was mistaken.

At Oritskys, I worked with a really nice guy named Manny. He was a "stacker," the guy who unloaded eight-foot bolts of fabric off the trucks and "stacked" them on the bolt holders so we "spreaders" could do our thing. It was backbreaking work, and one day Manny spoke up and demanded back braces for all the stackers in the factory. He tried to get a petition going in the union, but it did not go over well with management, and he was fired.

His firing seemed so unfair to me that I decided to do what my hero Caine would do. I attended the next union meeting, stood up, and spoke up in his defense. I was fired too.

Years later, I would read that actor David Carradine—who had played my hero, Caine—was found hanged in the closet of a Bangkok hotel with a cord wrapped around his neck and genitals, leading Thai police to suspect his death was not a suicide but an accident resulting from dangerous sex practices. This shocked and saddened me, as I realized that even the best of us have our demons.

I had to stop karate classes, as I no longer could afford the tuition, and more importantly, I had to find another job.

Of course every job application I filled out had questions. And one of the questions was always, "Have you ever been fired from a job?" and "If so, why?" I always told the truth, and I never got the jobs. By the sixth application, I decided to write "no" to that question and got hired that day.

I guess things happen for a reason, because the pay was almost double. The new job was at the Polymer Corporation, a manufacturer of precision plastic parts. And little did I know how working there would change the direction of my whole life.

"Never, ever, ever, ever, ever give up."

—Winston Churchill

CHAPTER 20

On Weiser Street in Reading, the row homes all had garages behind them that were connected to each other, just like the houses were. Everyone had a small patch of grass between the house and garage, where usually there resided a jumble of lawn chairs, charcoal grills, and whatnot.

Our neighbor, John, was a bit of a nut job. He was lawsuit crazy! If you ran into his garbage cans by mistake—lawsuit. If your bike bumped his car—lawsuit. He once sued me because I played my car stereo too loud. OK, that one was warranted.

But this one time, he really lost it. About 11:00 p.m., Loni and I came home from bowling. We stopped downstairs to pick up David from Mom and Charlie's and then hit the sack. I woke up about 3:00 a.m. to people yelling and pounding on the door downstairs and sirens coming up the alley. I smelled smoke and woke Loni, grabbed David, and ran downstairs to check on Mom and Charlie, still not realizing what had happened. By the time I got outside, the flames were engulfing my garage and were so hot the firemen were wetting down row homes nearby, having given up on the garage.

It burned completely to the ground, with only the melted shell of my beloved '67 Chevelle I had saved so hard for peeking through the ashes.

Turns out our litigious neighbor, John, had spent months filling his garage with old furniture, tools, and whatnot. Then he set it all on fire in the middle of the night, and burned my garage down too. We learned that after the fire, he made a large insurance claim for all of the old stuff in there. That shyster not only made a killing from his loss, he got rid of my loud car stereo too! I told the fire investigator that I knew John had started the fire, but they never found the cause, and no one worked very hard for justice in my neighborhood.

One week after the fire, Loni left me and took David.

• • • • •

I kind of understood it much later. We were both seventeen when we married, and I'm sure Loni felt she was missing out on a lot of fun stuff. Loni was pretty, with long blonde hair and soft looks. A few years later when I saw the movie *Forrest Gump,* I thought Loni looked just like Jenny. Loni worked evenings at Sammy's Steak Shop, and I had worried a bit when she started talking about a customer named Jerry who was a big tipper.

On the night Loni left, she just didn't come home. About three in the morning, I called her friend Shelley's house. Her mom answered and was not happy, but she woke Shelley up for me.

"Robbie, Loni is with Jerry." Shelley just told me straight up. She didn't even try to lie.

I also found out Jerry had been coming into my house when I was at work. I rode my bike over to Jerry's house and waited in the street outside. About an hour later, he came out on the porch with a cup of coffee and lit a cigarette. I got out and calmly climbed his stoop, punched him in the face as hard as I could, and broke his nose. "That's for coming into *my* house when I was at work!"

He never pressed charges. Perhaps taking my wife and son away from me was enough.

Mom and Charlie moved out. I sold the house on Weiser Street and paid Aunt Tilly back every penny.

ABOVE: THE OLD WOODWARD CAFÉ, READING, PENNSYLVANIA.

RIGHT: MY FIRST HOUSE, PURCHASED AT AGE 18 FOR $1000 DOWN.

CHAPTER 21

When Jeannie turned eighteen, Mom was notified by a letter from social services that Jeannie was moved from the sanitarium to a group home. I wanted to go see her, but Mom said it was *best to leave her be; she needed to learn to be on her own.*

Jeannie had more freedom at the group home, where she was allowed to take walks in the neighborhood alone. Jeannie was legally blind and had one eye with the pupil way off center, but otherwise I think she might have been pretty. She always had beautiful, thick, long hair—but they may have cut it in the institution.

The story goes she was out for a walk when this guy, Pete, approached her and asked for a cigarette. Then he asked where she lived and how old she was. This wasn't Pete's first rodeo with the group home residents, who he knew got steady Social Security checks. He told her he wanted to take her to lunch the next day—and "not to tell anyone." It would be their secret.

During their "date," Pete told Jeannie that she was legally able to leave the group home—and asked why she didn't just come live with him in his trailer and be his girlfriend. This sounded swell to Jeannie, who was never given a legal guardian—my mother never bothering with the paperwork. So off she went, and the State of Pennsylvania could go fuck themselves.

Of course the arrangement was all about Jeannie's government checks that arrived as regularly as Pete's beatings. That is until two years later, when our stepfather, Charlie, saw Pete's wedding announcement in the *Reading Eagle. And it wasn't to Jeannie.* Mom relented, and she and Charlie brought Jeannie home to live with them that very day.

Had Willie and Tom not been in prison, Pete would surely have been dead.

CHAPTER 22

When Loni left me and took David, I was broken. I decided to see a free therapist that my brother Tom had been ordered to see when he got out of juvie. *Finally, someone I could poor my aching heart out to.* And boy did I.

When I was finished, he looked at me closely and asked, "If you could do anything, Rob, anything at all, what would you do for fun?" I thought for a while.

"Motocross. I would ride motocross."

"Then do it!"

I did.

And you must have noticed by now that whatever I decided to do, I did it 200 percent. I raced every weekend I could find a competition, and when I wasn't at work, I would ride for hours at the practice course until I was so tired I couldn't hold my bike up. I started winning all the local races. I placed second in the Tri State Championships, even with a shitty bike. Competition was brutal, and you almost needed the latest and greatest in dirt bikes to win. I just didn't have the bucks, so I eventually sold my bike.

Once I had stopped riding and had no one to come home to, I decided to take my boss up on his offer of night school to get my Journeyman Machinist Toolmaker Certificate.

Engineers would come into the shop all the time for special tool designs, and it sure seemed to me they didn't know a lot of stuff. I would sometimes have to explain gently that their design would not work in the long haul, but if we made this small adjustment, it would probably pass the vigorous testing most companies required.

One day we were working on a particularly intricate and challenging machine when one of the shop guys came up behind me to watch. "Hey Rob, your left hand sure knows what your right hand is doing!"

He didn't know it, but that funny comment gave me the confidence to actually believe I might be able to go to college and study this stuff. I had been the only one of us five kids to even finish high school, and my grade average was a D when I did. But what the hell. I never let fear stop me before, so I wrote for an application to Penn State—and Ohio State too, since Loni and David were now living in Ohio with someone named Jim.

Penn State turned me down, but miraculously, I received a congratulations letter from Ohio State. *Hot damn, I was going to college.*

• • • • •

Six months later, I completed my Journeyman Toolmaker Certificate after four years of night classes. I sold what little I owned, including my beloved record collection and camera, saving the little profit from my house sale for tuition. When I said goodbye to Mom and Charlie, Mom reminded me that her brother, Billy, lived in Columbus. But I'd never met him; he was a stranger to me. She handed me a piece of paper with his phone number anyway.

I loaded what few possessions I had left into the trunk of the '73 Toyota Corolla I had bought after the garage fire and headed to Columbus, Ohio, scared out of my freaking mind. Outside of my one bus trip to visit my grandparents in Florida, I had never left the city. I hadn't opened a book since graduating Reading High, and I didn't know where I would sleep that night. I was twenty-five years old and starting college.

Well, not right away. I had to establish residency in Ohio first to qualify for in-state tuition. I needed a job. Thank goodness my boss wrote a nice letter about me that I kept in my wallet just in case.

As soon as I arrived in Columbus, I found my way to campus and bought a newspaper. I found a room advertised for $200 a month! I couldn't believe my luck. I figured I would put $100 down, find a job, and pay the rest after my first paycheck. I found a phone booth and called the number. No answer. Well, I decided *I'll eat one of the Lebanon Baloney sandwiches I packed and try again.* No answer. No answer. No answer. I found a twenty-four-hour McDonald's, washed up as best I could in the restroom, parked as far back as I could, and got into the back seat. I pulled some warmer clothes out of my Army surplus duffel and curled up, wondering what the fuck I was doing.

Someone did answer in the morning, and I was so grateful to get a response that I said I'd take the room without even seeing it. I stopped for some groceries, then took out my map to find the house. It was very close to campus, and I found it easily.

The house was a disaster. The porch was mostly rotted wood, and the front door wouldn't even close properly. Turns out the renter had placed the ad to help with expenses. I was told that if the landlord stopped by, I was to say I was "just a friend visiting." The room I was renting wasn't a bedroom at all but more of a utility closet without even a window. I could hear critters in the wall as I tried to sleep on the dirty single mattress someone had left behind.

I woke about 3:00 a.m. to the sound of my roommate in the shower. I got dressed, grabbed my duffel, tiptoed into his bedroom, retrieved my $100 from his wallet on the nightstand, and got the hell out of dodge.

• • • • •

Not knowing what else to do, I reluctantly called Uncle Billy. Uncle Billy and his partner, Jean, were never really married, according to my mom. Aunt Jean had been married to a doctor, had a very nice alimony check every month, and didn't want to fuck that up.

Uncle Billy and my mom hadn't spoken for years, but I pulled out the number she had written down for me. I waited until evening, found a phone booth, and stood in it for a long time before finally dialing the number. A lady answered, and I asked nervously, "May I speak to Billy?"

She asked, "Who is calling please?"

I just blurted out, "It's Rob. Rob Olsen. His nephew, Rob." Silence. This wasn't good.

Then I heard some muffled voices and almost hung up when a deep voice said loudly, "Bobby? Is this little Bobby?" I relaxed a little.

"Yes, Uncle Billy, but I go by Rob now." I don't recall much of what I said after that, I was so nervous, but I must have told him I was going to start college there and was so sorry to ask, but could

I stay with him for a night or two until I found a room. I held my breath.

I heard him say, "Of course you can, Bobby! Come right now!"

My mother rarely spoke of her family, so I was surprised to find that Uncle Billy was so handsome! He looked just like Pete Carroll, coach of the Seattle Seahawks. Uncle Billy had played football in high school, just like Pete, and had no shortage of female attention. I found out years later that Uncle Billy even dated my father's sister, my Aunt Louise! He was funny too, and made me feel welcome.

But nothing is ever perfect, and I soon found out he was an alcoholic like Mom. A mean drunk, the worst kind. Thoughts of Jack came flooding back, causing me great distress, so I would make myself scarce in the evening before they came home. Jean drank too, and they would have the ugliest fights, then act like nothing had happened in the morning.

But Aunt Jean was educated. "A highly respected English teacher," Uncle Billy said. And cultured. And generous. And elegant. I never saw her in a pair of slacks. She played beautiful music in the house. She loved the symphony and the opera. They had an extensive library too. I found out she had a masters in English literature, and always had a book in her hands. One day she knocked on my bedroom door carrying a small, blue book. "You should read this." She laid it on the dresser and closed the door.

I'm not exaggerating one iota when I say I'm not a reader. Not even close. If it wasn't an instruction manual of some kind, I never had the time. I had read only one storybook. Why I didn't read, I can't answer; but here was Aunt Jean, book in hand, and I figured I kind of had to read it.

I walked over to the dresser and picked it up. *Siddhartha*, by Herman Hesse. It was a small book, not many pages. There was a dreamy drawing on the cover of a mystical-looking horse and a mysterious woman adorned with jewels and a head wrap. I tossed it on the bed and went out to wax my car.

With Aunt Jean's help, I found out that I could start classes in only six months with in-state tuition. She was an alumna, and I guessed "it's who ya know," as they say. Now, with my newly-minted Journeyman Toolmaker Certificate in hand, I put on my best shirt, grabbed the phone book, and headed out.

With the letter of recommendation from the Polymer Corporation in Reading, I landed a job on the spot with a small tool and dye shop west of campus.

I was seldom home, working overtime as much as I could, but I was usually home on weekends. One day, Aunt Jean surprised me with tickets to a play at The Ohio Theatre. I borrowed a tie from Uncle Billy, and Aunt Jean and I headed out to the theater in my Corolla. She asked me to drop her in front of the theater, then I drove a few blocks to find free parking, and hustled back to meet her.

My God this place is beautiful, I told myself as I walked in. An opulent, Spanish, baroque-style exterior led to a lush interior full of velvet-fringed drapery and hundreds of rows of green velvet seats. In the middle was a 21-foot crystal chandelier that I had never seen the likes of. High up on the sides of the theater were private, little Juliet balconies. I borrowed Aunt Jean's binoculars to see that they were full of beautiful people. One man even had on a tuxedo.

Aunt Jean told me that in its heyday, the theater had lavish men's and women's lounge areas, including separate smoking and telephone rooms! Over $1 million was spent on furnishings alone, more than the cost of the building. But I think what impressed me the most was when she told me that the Grateful Dead, Frank

Zappa, and Alice Cooper had all graced the stage! It was quite a night for a kid from the Mission.

My aunt and uncle were generous in so many ways, but some things really bothered me. Aunt Jean sometimes spoke in double meanings, or spoke words I didn't understand. It was usually when drinking, and I think just to fuck with me. And like I said, Uncle Billy was a mean drunk—which seemed so strange, because he was on the quiet side when sober.

I decided to leave after an especially ugly fight. Uncle Billy had trashed the living room furniture with an axe from the garage. Really. It brought back memories of you-know-who, and well, enough said. By morning, I was packed up. They were still sleeping it off when I tiptoed down the stairs, placing the note I had written explaining that I was leaving but was "very grateful to them" on the kitchen table. I took one last look around, then quietly closed the back door.

I was distressed to find I had forgotten to grab my new student information folder. I waited a few hours, then called them. Uncle Billy asked me to stop back over before I got a chance to tell him I had left something behind. When I arrived, he gave me the biggest hug and all of his drafting tools, which I still have today.

As I was backing out of their driveway Aunt Jean hurried down the drive and handed me two books. "Read these too, Rob," she told me, and, "You can keep them."

"Thank you, Aunt Jean," I answered, and added, "and thanks for everything. It meant a lot to me." She smiled, turned, and joined Uncle Billy on the porch, both waving until I was out of sight.

At the first red light, I read the book covers: *Catcher in the Rye* and *The Good Earth*. I later read and loved them both.

CHAPTER 23

I found a room for rent on the edge of campus. It was owned by a grad student, Doug Bachman—a tall, lanky guy who designed retail store interiors for The Duty Company in Columbus. He had borrowed $10,000 from his mom for a down payment and needed a tenant to help with the mortgage payment.

Doug's German girlfriend, Gisela, soon joined us. Tall, blonde and elegant like Doug, they looked like Nordic royalty. This pained me greatly, as my own insecurities about my bad teeth and old clothes consumed me. I was still very unsure of myself, feeling that I didn't really belong there, and soon everyone else would know too.

It must have showed. Doug and Gisela were especially kind to me, and would gently guide me a bit when I stumbled in dress and speech. An especially painful incident occurred when Doug had a few friends over one night. I had a lab the next morning, so I went to bed early. One of his guests used the bathroom across from my room and left the door and bright light on when they left. I called out, "Please outen the lights!" A few seconds later, I heard laughter coming from the living room. There was no doubt it was at my expense. I realized that I had picked up many words from the Mennonites—and that no one talked like me in Ohio.

The next day Gisela suggested I just say, "Hit the lights." I didn't mind her feedback. I was grateful actually, desperate not to draw attention to myself.

Gisela would sometimes help me dress for a date. I had never gone out with a college girl, and wasn't at all sure that I was ready. That proved true one evening when my date suggested we stop by a pre-game tailgate party. I was too shy to ask what a tailgate party was, but soon we were drinking beer off a tailgate in a packed parking lot with a lot of happy people. Things were going well, and I started to feel pretty good, when some people started arguing about Woody this and why didn't Woody do that.

"Who is Woody?" I asked. Silence. I mean deafening.

"You're kidding, right?" All eyes turned to me, and I prayed for someone to just shoot me.

My date laughed, "Of course he's kidding! Come on, Rob; let's take a walk." We didn't go back to the tailgate, and I told her I had to work in the morning and better get home.

When I got home, Doug told me Woody Hayes was the three-time winner of Football Coach of the Year and a legend at Ohio State.

• • • • •

One day, Doug brought home a flyer from campus. "Here Rob, you should look into this. Looks like a good deal." It was all about the Ohio State Dental School. How they offered dental care to students at huge discounts. The dental students would work on you, with an instructor supervising. I had only been to a dentist twice in my life. Both times in The Mission, both times to have a tooth pulled. I thanked Doug and tucked the flyer in my backpack.

I didn't want to show my teeth to anyone. Not even a dentist. Or a dental student. But it pained me even more to look at my mouth, so I signed up. And it took a dental student named Malone all four years to rebuild my mouth.

In the early eighties, the US economy began to tank, and I found myself without a job. The small tool and die I worked for just could not afford to keep everyone. For the first time in my life, I filed for unemployment benefits.

I was thrilled to have more time to study and work on my car. I started helping Doug set up retail displays, getting paid under the table. And Uncle Billy would call me to fix stuff at his house—always paying me generously. Along with my unemployment checks, I was making more money than ever, and had more spare time to boot!

Loni and David were living in Athens, just an hour and a half from Columbus, so with more spare time I drove there to see David every other weekend. Loni's boyfriend, Jim, was on the quiet side, and I was surprised to learn that he had a master's degree and worked at Ohio University. He was always gracious to me when I visited, even suggesting I spend the night when it got late one evening and the roads were icy.

I always had to be back in Columbus by Monday morning. You see, there was one problem with my sweet work situation. The unemployment office made you look for work every week. I mean, they actually gave you names of places you had to apply to. If you didn't follow the rules, they eliminated your benefits.But I had a plan. I'd go to the interviews and always tell them I had classes during the times they needed someone.

One day, they sent me to a plastic fabricating company called Plaskolite. Established in 1950, its first success was in production of hula-hoops, flyswatters, and florescent lighting panels. At this point, they made large thermoplastic sheeting used in things like shower enclosures and plexiglass.I really didn't want the job, so I showed up for my interview in ratty jeans and a lumberjack shirt. I told them my class hours were all over the place, and they would have to work around those. And I asked for five dollars an hour more than they were offering.

To my complete shock, they said OK. I started that Monday.

After a few weeks of work, I noticed something that just didn't feel right. They had a system of heating large 4-by-8-foot thermoplastic sheets used in shower enclosures in a large vacuum-forming machine only to bend a 1/8th inch straight line through the middle of the sheet. It seemed like overkill to me.

It's kind of strange, but most of my ideas would come to me in dreams. One night, I dreamed of a small machine that would heat only the 1/8th inch part, not heating the whole sheet. When I woke up, I sketched my idea on a notepad and took it into my boss. He showed it to the owner, and sure enough, they let me build it. It saved both time and mucho moolah. It should have been my first patent, but the owner said we were a small company and couldn't afford a patent attorney and the fees.

• • • • •

One day, Doug asked if I wanted to drive with them to New York City to drop Gisela off at the airport for a flight back to Germany to visit her folks. It felt like the perfect break from classes and work, so I said yes.

After we dropped her off, Doug suggested we park somewhere

and we grabbed our bikes out of the trunk to explore the city. I had never been to Manhattan and thought this was a great idea. Doug had heard about a famous pizza place in Greenwich Village called Joe's Pizza, so off we rode through the crowded streets like two maniacs on a mission. It was the best damn pizza I ever tasted, and I had grown up in an Italian neighborhood!

We had both heard a lot about the fabled Harlem, so with map in hand, we rode about eight miles into a place that seemed like a different planet. Gone were the hipster coffee shops, amazing bakeries, and quirky boutiques. This was heartbreaking. We rode past junkies on every street corner, boarded-up apartment buildings, and faces without hope on door stoops. A group of young men gathered on the corner we were headed for. I turned back to look at Doug, riding just behind me.

I could see he was terrified, all color draining from his already pale face. *Shit, this is just like my neighborhood back home, as comfortable to me as my favorite socks,* I thought. Still, we rode like hell out of Harlem, slowing down only a second to take a picture of the Apollo Theatre.

We threw our bikes in the trunk, jumped in the car, and got the heck out of dodge—laughing all the way to Columbus.

Gisela never came back, and, well, I left soon too.

I was rarely home. When not in class, I was in the library studying, or at work. But one night I was home, and Doug suggested we go out and grab a beer. I thought it was because I was still hurting terribly from a recent breakup, but I soon found it wasn't about me at all.

We sat down at the long bar, Doug choosing the quieter end. We were enjoying our beers when Doug turned to me. I could see he was nervous about something.

"Rob, what's the worst thing I could tell you right now?"

"Huh? What are you talking about?" He just looked at me, not answering. And then it hit me. Like a ton of bricks. So many little things, things I ignored, or chose not to see. "No, you're not. Get the fuck out. You're kidding, right? For real? Shit." But I could tell it was for real. Doug was gay.

Now I loved this guy, more than my own brothers. I tried to make it work, living there I mean. But I guess like some gay guys when they first come out, Doug went a little crazy. He completely changed the way he dressed—and even talked. He started having wild parties, so I stayed even later in the library on the nights I wasn't working. But the last straw was when I came home one night, exhausted after a hard shift, and found two guys going at it in my bed! Doug was mortified and explained that they mistook my room for the guest room, but the damage was done.

I moved out the next day, but I never forgot his kindness, and we remain friends to this day. I visited Doug and his longtime partner, Steve, in their million-dollar home in Fort Lauderdale last year.

"How hard can it be?"

—My friend Judd.

CHAPTER 24

I found a spacious room for rent about fifteen minutes from campus. It was owned by another engineering student, so I knew there wouldn't be a lot of partying, and I even had my own bathroom. One Sunday, I decided to take a drive out to a nearby reservoir I had heard about on Old State Line Road. It was a beautiful day, and I just couldn't bear studying indoors.

I headed north, following my roommate's directions, and was soon driving through rolling farmland only thirty minutes from campus. I rounded a curve and saw the most beautiful lake peeking through the trees. "Alum Creek State Park," the sign said. I pulled into the parking lot, a bit disappointed to see so many cars. *No worries, I thought.* I would hike until I found a quiet spot.

I grabbed my backpack and headed out, gazing up at the dark shale cliffs that lined the irregular shore. I rounded a corner and found a perfect little sandy beach. I sat down to study, when something out in the lake caught my eye.

It was clear across the lake, and I could hardly make it out, but it looked like someone had put a sail on a surfboard, was standing on it, and moving along pretty damn fast! I shut my book and stood up, straining to see what the heck it was, when it suddenly turned on a dime and headed in the other direction! OK, the hell with studying, I had to see this thing. I packed up and hurried back to my car, finding my way to the other side of the reservoir.

The lake was big, and by the time I got there, the man and his board were sitting on the shore.

"What the heck is that?" I blurted out in my excitement.

"It's a windsurfer," he answered.

"Did you make it yourself?"

"Nope, bought it from a guy who bought it in California. It's the rage there."

I learned his name was Don Dunphey, and that he wrote computer software. Funny, I had a quick mental flash of him working on huge computers like Hal from *2001: A Space Odyssey*. This was the early 1980s, and he was the only software engineer I knew of.

He was maybe ten years older than me and generous as all-get-out. He offered to teach me, and we started meeting at the lake every weekend. I learned that it is not easy to learn to windsurf. It takes balance and strength, adjusting to changing wind and waves, knowing what size sail is correct for the current conditions, holding your sail in just the right spot—all while trying to stand and not run into anyone or anything.

But I was determined, and Don was patient—so soon I was sailing along with confidence.

One day, Don showed up with a second board on top of his car. He had a friend who had bought a board but lost interest. I eagerly bought his friend's board and took it out that same day. Now I could windsurf whenever I could find the time, and boy did I find the time.

It became almost an obsession. When I wasn't at work or in class, I was at Alum Creek on my board in every kind of weather, determined to master the jibe and some jumps.

Don said he thought I was getting good enough to race and invited me to join him in a race that very weekend in Cleveland.

Racing with Don was a blast. One day, we were at the reservoir practicing high wind tacks and jibes. We knew a storm was approaching and hoped to get in at least an hour of practice. We were so busy hootin' and hollerin' in the crazy wind that we didn't see the storm had strengthened and was almost upon us. It started raining like hell, and we couldn't see each other though the pelting rain—although I knew we were only yards apart.

All of a sudden I felt the hair on my body stand up and heard Don yell, "JUMP! GET INTO THE FUCKING WATER NOW!"

I jumped just as the biggest lightning bolt I had ever seen hit the lake right in front of us. Had we been on our boards, we would surely have been killed, as an aluminum sailboard mast is the perfect conductor.

Boy did we need a drink after nearly being fried to death, so we stopped at a pub near the lake to have a stiff one and collect ourselves, kidding about our near miss. Then suddenly, I don't know why, I never did this, but I told Don about my years in the orphanage. Maybe because he was older and had a wife and kids and a good job. He was kind of a role model for me.

He listened carefully to my telling, staying silent, and I swear his eyes misted up. Then he surprised me by standing up from his barstool and giving me a huge, embarrassingly-long bear hug. Then he sat back down, and we didn't say another word. He insisted on paying, and we walked out to our cars with his arm around my shoulders.

Don and I continued to sail together until I graduated and moved up north, but I never forgot his kind friendship.

CHAPTER 25

I had a heavy schedule in the fall of '82: two labs, differential equations, and a chemical engineering class. My engineering class professor gave a quiz every day before class. I usually had an hour before class to study, but one day my car wouldn't start, and by the time I rode my bike to the far side of campus, he was handing out the quiz. *Shit.* Sometimes there was just one question, and damn, wouldn't you know this was one of those days.

"Define 'Piezo Resistance.'" Hmmm…might as well go for broke.

I wrote, "When Dominos is reluctant to deliver pizza to your house. Piezo Resistance!" Then I apologized, explained that I was working two jobs, going to school full-time—including two tough labs, *which no one in their right mind would do*—and my car had broken down that morning.

I turned in my paper, then quietly walked over to the lab tables to work on a lab assignment with those who had finished the quiz. I had always used humor as a child when I didn't know what else to do, and I hoped it might work in this situation. I was watching the professor out of the corner of my eye, and peeked over just in time to see him jerk his head up and look quickly and curiously around the room. I was grateful he had no idea who I was—it was a large class—and thankfully, he didn't call me out. After class, we picked up our quizzes. He gave me a C for my goofy joke of an answer!After class I really should have gone home to get some sleep, but instead decided to find out where a "robot" that all the engineering students were talking about was being built. I found it in one of the engineering buildings, surrounded by a bunch of students. I couldn't believe what I was looking at.

"What the fuck?" I said a little too loudly.

"Yeah, I know," answered one of the students. "Pretty cool." There in front of me were two super-tall—maybe seven feet high—mechanical "legs," topped by two huge boxes holding computers, and between the legs a steel "cage" of sorts where a single operator would sit at the controls. It looked like something straight out of *Star Wars.*

"It's an Adaptive Suspension Vehicle," the student informed me. "We're building it for the US Army!" He went on to explain that they were volunteers—science and engineering students—working with Professors Robert McGhee and Kenneth Waldron. "It will have six legs when finished, be able to step over obstacles as tall as seven feet, and traverse trenches as wide as twenty-three feet," he explained.

Damn. I just had to get on this team. Then reality set in. I simply had no time. I was already behind in my schoolwork, and couldn't afford to cut back my work hours.

I was a bit down as I left the group and was heading out when I noticed a door at the end of a short hall to my left. What caught my eye were the words "ANECHOIC CHAMBER," and "KEEP DOOR

LOCKED." I turned and walked down the hall. I had read about these chambers and didn't realize the university had one. No one was around, so I tried the door. It opened.

I was surprised to find a very large room with a smaller—maybe twenty-foot square room—within it. A kind of room within a room. *So this must be the anechoic chamber.* The door to the chamber was very large, like a big walk-in safe. I moved closer and pulled the door open. It was very heavy and about two feet thick! The room was dark, so I felt for a light switch, found it, and turned on a dim ceiling light. The room was surprisingly large, with a single chair in the middle. I turned to see that no one was around and went in, closing the door behind me.

I sat down in the chair, closed my eyes, and listened. After a few minutes of silence, I thought I could detect the slightest sound from the light fixture above. I got up, turned off the light, then walked carefully in complete darkness and felt for the chair. I sat down again, eyes open, and listened. Nothing. And I mean deafening silence. It was very strange at first.

But after what I guessed was only a few minutes, I felt something. The silence felt good. I started to experience a detachment from the world and a heightened sense of reality. I felt a strange sense of what I can only describe as completeness. I once read that a fractured thing craves wholeness. That when you break a bone, healing begins in seconds. The body needs to feel complete. I sat in this delicious completeness maybe fifteen minutes more, then thought I better leave before I was found.

The next time I visited the campus library, I looked up *anechoic chambers* and read that they are indeed the quietest place on earth. According to the *Smithsonian Magazine*, an anechoic chamber at Orfield Laboratories in Minnesota is so quiet that the longest anybody has been able to bear it is forty-five minutes.

I left the library thinking that surely I could stay longer than that. I felt my younger self had been there before me. The silence and safety of my childhood pine tree forest was my anechoic chamber.

And about that robot Ohio State was building, years later I learned that after spending ten years and millions of dollars, the government decided it was too slow and cumbersome and abandoned the whole project. The robot is rumored to still be in storage somewhere on campus, dejected and forgotten.

CHAPTER 26

By now, all those hours in the dental chair were beginning to pay off, and I finally had the confidence to approach a girl in my physics class named Katie and ask for a date. I'd had a bit of a crush on her for about a year but heard her father was a big-time Columbus lawyer, and well, that made me hesitate.

I dialed her dorm room. No answer. *What the heck?* I called back and left a message, hung up, then wished I could erase it. I had no idea what I had just said.

A few days later, she called me! Her father had given her tickets to the Columbus Symphony, and she asked if I would like to go. "Yehudi Menuhin is the guest violinist," she said, and, "What a thrill that he is in Columbus!" I agreed, trying to hide the fact that I had no idea who he was.

I loved it so much. His hauntingly beautiful and sad violin instantly transported me back to The Mission and my young, lonely heart. It moved me to tears, and I just couldn't hold them back, which caused me some distress—until I noticed other people dabbing their eyes with tissues as well.

I had one more date with Katie before she called one night and asked just to be friends. I was crushed. I never called her again.

• • • • •

Graduation was quickly approaching, and I was busy studying for finals, but something had been on my mind. I felt I needed to go over to the dental school and thank Dr. Malone for saving my teeth. He was graduating too, same as me. After a year or so in his chair, I confided in him that I was the only one in my family to still have teeth.

I remember my mom being very young when she came home with a toothless grin. "With the price the dentist gave me to fix my teeth, I said, 'Hell no—just pull what's left!'" Despite later feeling badly about it, I was ashamed of her appearance until she could afford ill-fitting dentures.

I was happy to see Dr. Malone was working the day I stopped by. He made time to see me. "Rob, I'm so glad you stopped by. I wanted to invite you to my dental school graduation party. Honestly, Rob, I've never seen anyone change as much as you have from the first time you walked into the clinic. I'm afraid to say it, but I thought you were just some guy trying to sneak in! I didn't believe you were a student here. I've watched you change through the years, and I'd like you to be a guest at my graduation party next week."

There are no words. OK, maybe gobsmacked. I mean I just wanted to *drink in this moment*. To remember this feeling forever. I felt a thickness in my throat as I tried to answer. I was starting to belong.

He handed me an invitation in an envelope with a gold seal. I waited until I got home to open it. There was a card inside someone had handwritten in the most beautiful cursive, with a raised gold border, all protected by a gold square of tissue paper. When the day came, I shaved and put on the new sport coat I had purchased for the engineering school job fair, polished my shoes, and combed my hair carefully.

Then I took it all off. I didn't go. I just couldn't. My fear of not knowing what to do or say was just too much.

Mom and Charlie drove in from Reading for my graduation, and I'd never seen Mom so proud. The three of us went to dinner after, and they headed back to Reading the next day.

I had attended an engineering school job fair the month before graduation, and after two weeks of waiting, I received a job offer from a large company called Owens Illinois (OI) based in Toledo, Ohio. I was hoping they would call, because I knew Toledo sat on Lake Erie, and I had raced there several times with Don and loved its sandy shores.

I was beyond shocked to find out I was offered more money than any other mechanical engineering school graduate in the history of Ohio State. My professor said it was because I was also a journeyman toolmaker with an invention to my name. He said most of my fellow students had never worked in engineering—and certainly had never invented something.

The very next day, I went to the bank, showed them my job offer, and was given a $6,000 loan on the spot. One of my conditions accepting the offer from OI was not to start work for six weeks.

I was totally burned out. It took everything I had to finish school, and I knew I needed a rest. The bank loan allowed me to take a real vacation, with plenty left over for a deposit and first month's rent for a place in Toledo.

I said goodbye to Doug and his partner, Steve; packed a few belongings; gave away the rest; tied my windsurfer to the top of my

VW Rabbit (I rotated through cars a few times in those days!); and headed for the San Francisco Bay. I'd always dreamed of windsurfing that crazy wind under the Golden Gate Bridge, and, well, for the first time in my life, there was nothing to stop me.

"Just do it!"

—Nike

CHAPTER 27

You gotta be brave before you can be good.

The Golden Gate Bridge loomed high above, as I gazed out at the choppy bay, the likes of which I had never seen. I'd windsurfed in all kinds of conditions and wave types, but this was different.

There are two kinds of water here. The Bay water is runoff from the surrounding land. It is warmer and carries silt. But the Pacific Ocean is cold, stirred by upwellings and tides. This creates a perfect storm of sorts, resulting in turbulent, dangerous, ever-changing wave patterns. It is considered one of the most unusual places to go windsurfing on the planet.

And that, my friends, is why I'm standing here.

The day I arrived was cold and foggy. Only a handful of radicals were out, and they were playing it safe, staying close to shore.

Still, I was beyond excited. The forecast for the rest of the week was sunny and unusually mild for late spring, perfect for first-timers. I pulled on my fleece jacket and sat down on the rocky shore to watch. These guys were good. They were doing maneuvers I had never seen. And the point breaks!

Maybe I should explain. A point break is where a wave breaks as it hits a point of land jutting out from the coastline. On top of that, the large bridge supports in the Bay played all kinds of havoc. Not to mention freighters and all manner of sea-faring vessels passing under the bridge that the surfers had to watch for. I just had to talk to these guys, so I walked down the shore a bit to where I saw their gear to wait for them. When I got a look at their beautiful equipment and top-notch spare boards, harnesses, and booms, I turned around and went back to my rocky perch.

I had pretty shitty equipment, and my wetsuit was even sadder. There was no way I was showing up with my stuff. So with $6,000 burning a hole in my pocket, I headed to a popular windsurf shop in the city I had read about in *Windsurf Magazine.* Funny, as I drove over the famous bridge, the thadud…thadud…thadud of vehicles speeding across the highway grates was deafening.

But underneath the bridge, it was a different world. All one hears is wind and water. I couldn't wait to get back there.

The shop was easy to find, as the parking lot was filled with funky old cars topped with colorful surfing gear—and all sorts of quirky people in wild shirts and shorts laughing and carrying on. *Welcome to California.*

When I walked out, I was the proud owner of a bright red, Rip Curl wetsuit and a spanking new Mistral sail. It was the most money I had ever spent on myself, outside of my $10,000 rowhome. I drove back to the bay, elated with my new gear.

That lasted about twenty minutes, before second thoughts about my extravagant purchase began haunting me. What was I thinking? I was a poor boy from Reading, Pennsylvania's, inner city. I tried to shake it off, not wanting to spoil my dream trip. Heck, I had a big fat salary awaiting me in Toledo. Still, these thoughts were something I would struggle with the rest of my life.

It was getting late, and I'd heard you could pitch a tent at nearby Kirby Cove for a small fee, so I found my way there and set up for the night. Some other campers told me about a nearby carry-out, so I picked up two slices of hours-old pizza and a soda, drove back, and fell asleep minutes after scarfing down my dinner.

In the morning, I was feeling pretty confident in my new gear and couldn't wait to join the other surfers already well out into the bay. The wind was a bit more than I had hoped for, but the sun was shining, and the sky clear.

There was a small beach between the rocks, and I took off from there, the wind filling my sail within seconds. I was cautious at first, letting the sail out until I felt stable. There would be no jumps for me today, the waves and wind so unfamiliar. Soon, I got the feel of these strange wave patterns and was sailing confidently, even keeping up with the radicals. Then it hit me: *what a great place to learn how to water start!* A water start is when you start windsurfing laying in the water, not from the shore. It's hard to learn, but important to know how to do if you are sailing in high winds on a "short" board, and fall off into the water.

I had always wanted to learn, but it's hard, and I just never took the time. Now I had the time, and this strong wind was perfect! You start by treading water, staying close to your board, reaching up and emptying your sail of any water, positioning the mast perpendicular to the wind, lifting the luff (forward edge of the sail) out of the water, and allowing the wind to catch the sail. Then hopefully the wind will be enough to fill the sail and pull you out of the water and onto your board at the same time it starts moving forward.

All this happens in a matter of seconds, if all goes well. Occasionally a rider may be unable to water start if the wind has dropped. If this happens and you are on a small sinker board (a board that will sink when you stand on it if you aren't moving), you are in deep shit. Even if you are able to climb onto your board, it is so small that it will stay submerged several feet.

But my board was large, so I could always hoist myself up out of the deep water if the wind calmed. I sailed to a good spot out of the path of the boat traffic and slipped into the cold water, holding tightly to the boom. I positioned myself perfectly, but just could not lift the sail up from this position to catch enough wind. I kept trying, almost getting up, but then quickly sinking back down into the sea. Learning to water start is really tough.

I noticed another windsurfer heading my way at great speed. I thought maybe he knew me, as he was staring at me as he approached. He slowed enough to shout, "Are you OK?"

Hmmm.... "YES!" I yelled, "I'm fine!"

He jibed and came around again. "Hey man, are you SURE you're OK?"

I gave him a thumbs up, but he didn't smile back. I thought I saw him shake his head as he took off to join the others.

After a few more unsuccessful tries, I was getting tired and pulled myself up onto my board, lifted the sail, and took off instantly, deciding to sail under the bridge one more time before calling it a day. The shadow of the bridge darkened the water, and for a moment I thought I was seeing things. But I wasn't. I was heading straight for a large fin sticking out of the water, crossing a few yards in front of me. In a split second all the pieces came together. *Sharks.* That's what the guy was trying to warn me about, asking if I was sure I was OK.

ABOVE: MOTOCROSS

LEFT: COLUMBIA RIVER GORGE NEAR HOOD RIVER, OREGON.

PLEASEGODPLEASEGODPLEASEGOD don't let me fall. I held on tight as my board broadsided the shark. Miraculously, I stayed on my board by throwing my weight to one side before leveling out again. I was beyond terrified but managed to carefully jibe and head back to the nearest shore I could find.

I pulled my board in and sat down on dry land, my heart still beating so hard it shook my whole body. *HOLYSHITHOLYSHITHOLYSHIT.....*I made myself take a few deep breaths and tried to calm myself down. As my heartbeat began to quiet, I realized I had pissed in my new wetsuit.

I didn't mind leaving a bit of my heart in San Fran, but an arm or leg was out of the question. I hurried back to my tent, packed up, and headed down the coast to California—grateful to be alive.

Two days later on my car radio as I was heading south along the coast, I heard a windsurfer was badly bitten by a shark in the Frisco Bay.

It was a beautiful drive down the California coast. I made a small detour north to see the redwoods, and it brought back memories of my time in the forest as a child—finding comfort there when there was none for me in the world.

CHAPTER 28

I continued to race, mostly on Lake Erie, and when I was transferred to Lakeland, Florida, I windsurfed almost every day after work. I started winning every race I entered, so I got up the courage to sign up for nationals. This was a big deal, because the top qualifiers would go on to the Olympic Trials.

That year, nationals were in Miami, so I wouldn't even have to travel far. One to always pinch a penny, I heard that you could camp at a nearby marina for a small fee—so I was all set.

The night before the race, I had a pasta dinner with some friends before heading off to my tent early so I could get a good night's sleep. *Not.*

Now I really should have thought about this, I thought. In most marinas, there are sailboats. Sailboats have masts. Masts with all kinds of gear hanging from them. Gear that clangs with the slightest wind. It was impossible to sleep, even with my head wrapped in anything I could find to dull the constant clang. I woke tired and irritated. I was edgy and had a false start, costing me a place on our USA Windsurfing Team.

One day my boss came into my office and told me I was being transferred back to Toledo. I wasn't surprised; it's where Owens Illinois was headquartered. I told my boss I didn't want to go. I loved living in Florida. But he explained to me that if I didn't take the transfers offered to me, I would never be promoted. I really had no choice.

I reluctantly took the transfer, and this time instead of renting, I bought a small house with a large garage in Perrysburg, Ohio—a suburb of Toledo. At least I'd be closer to David. I felt badly that I hadn't seen him much living in Florida.

Just a few weeks after I settled into my new house, David called. "Dad, can I come live with you?"

I was surprised, although he had mentioned the idea to me a few times in the past. I froze for a moment. I wasn't sure I even knew how to be a parent. The few weeks we spent together every year were mostly on his summer vacation, which was very different than raising a child full-time. David was fourteen now, a moody teenager. I thought about my own longing for a father at that age.

"Of course you can, son!" I heard myself say. "If it's OK with your mom."

It was, and I picked him up that weekend.

I taught him to work with tools, fix his bike, change the oil in my car—and together we built a new trailer to haul my boards.

I taught him to windsurf too, and we would travel together to race all over the Great Lakes. And every Christmas when he was on break, we would pack up our boards and head to the Florida Keys for two weeks.

The time with David seemed to fly by, and I realized he would be heading to college next year. We both knew this was probably our last Florida Keys trip together.

We were both unusually quiet on the drive down—and later I'd realize it was more than melancholy.

"Do one thing every day that scares you."

—Eleanor Roosevelt

CHAPTER 29

Did you know that barracudas are ferocious predators? Relying on surprise and short bursts of speed, up to 36 miles an hour, they overtake their prey quickly and then bite them in half. *Kinda wish I would have known this.*

They are snake-like in appearance with razor-sharp, fang teeth—much like the piranha—all in different sizes, set in sockets in their large, powerful jaws. Like sharks, some barracudas will attack humans, although such incidents are rare. *I was one of those rare incidents.*

The Florida Keys, mile marker 39. Between Missouri Key and Bahia Honda lies Ohio Key. It is also known as Sunshine Key after a campground there that takes up about half of the small island. The southern half is a protected wildlife sanctuary full of palm trees, mangroves, buttonwoods, and birdwatchers. My windsurfing buds and I had been camping there every December for years.

We were a motley crew for sure. Not much in common save a fierce love of windsurfing, big waves, and warm sunshine.

There was Derk and Donna, who were the oldest in the group. Derk built racing engines and was probably the quietest. Donna was a wonderful cook, spoiling us each night with some amazing dessert creation. They lived on Lake Erie along with their son, Paul, a carpenter who also raced. They had another son we called Wall Street. In finance, he showed up one day at the Windsurf Club BBQ wearing a suit and tie, cuff links even! He said he surfed, but no one actually ever saw him on a board.

Terry and his wife, Sally, were regulars. Terry worked for the railroad but seemed to be perpetually laid off. He would do all kinds of odd jobs and had a talent for talking people into giving him free stuff. I wasn't surprised to hear that he had moved into the Florida condo of one of his customers when they had vacated to go north for the summer. No charge! And he always showed up to Sunshine Campground without much food or equipment, joking about it as he and Sally settled in, asking what time lunch was!

Kip, a chiropractor; and his wife, Ann, who sold pharmaceuticals; were a great couple who sometimes would bring their kids down. They always pitched their tent away from the group, being good parents and all.

Then there was Kenny who owned the windsurfing shop in town. A small man with a Hitler-like mustache that drove David nuts, he raced more than anyone until his heart attack at eighty.

Tall, handsome, chick magnet Evan—another carpenter—rounded out our little band of unlikely, high-wind lovin', radical surfers.

In December of 91', our group headed down to Sunshine Campground, knowing it would be the last group trip there for many of us. With David leaving for college soon, I was happy we would have this time together. I'd always been bothered by the fact that I wasn't around much before he came to live with me three years prior, and I suddenly felt a strong need to be with him.

We spent our days surfing, sunning, grilling, laughing, and drinking—each of us knowing how special this really was. Some were slowing down, others were moving, kids were growing. In January, I would be turning thirty-six, and I wasn't sure how many racing years were ahead for me.

• • • • •

One clear, warm night, the marine weather station out of Key West buzzed with an alert while we were just leaving the campfire for bed: Tropical storm! High winds! Expect 40- to 50 mile-an-hour gusts for the Florida Keys! Wave heights 5 to 6, winds starting tomorrow at 11:00 a.m. Eastern. Repeat—high wind warning! Near hurricane force winds possible!

Hot damn.

We got up early to begin tying things down, securing tents and equipment, checking the forecast, scarfing down breakfast, and yes—pulling on our wet suits. We figured we had two good hours of surfing before the storm hit. Our camping neighbors looked curiously on as they packed up campsites frantically and skedaddled.

The six of us rigged up our short boards quickly. No way were the girls going out on the water. Everyone's adrenaline was on overdrive, and we nervously joked about ending up in Cuba as we pulled our boards out for a water start.

Dear Lord, we were fast. *Scary fast. I was in heaven.*

However, it is super exhausting to sail in these conditions for long, so soon we were down to four—then down to two, myself and Terry. I tried to maneuver close to Terry, and when I saw his face, I knew he was done too. We headed back, exhausted and beyond thrilled. Cold beer and snacks awaited us as we struggled out of our wet suits.

Everyone hunkered down on the beach, bundled in warm blankets and ski jackets, save for me. I was just aching to do one more run out to a tiny island about a mile from camp. It held no buildings and no people, and not even a good landing spot. But no worries, I didn't plan on staying. With this wind and the smallest sail I owned—my 2.7—I figured I'd be there and back before the big wind hit. Of course, bets were made on the crazy bastard (me), to see if I could make it back before the storm blew me to Oz.

Holy moly! This was wind the pros only dream about. I figured I had maybe thirty minutes. If I had any chance of making it, it had to be on my Jimmy Lewis.

Jimmy was the premium board maker in the 1980s. Having built his first board as a teenager in his garage, his boards were the choice of champions, breaking speed records around the world. Of course I bought it used, never could afford a new one. My Jimmy was a sinker, so I would need to get moving—FAST—to keep it from plunging me into the water. Water starts only, high-wind conditions. Only highly-skilled surfers would attempt to use a sinker like that, and not all of them would succeed. Forty mile-an-hour minimum wind was required. *Check, check and check.*

I scarfed down a beer and a handful of pretzels, grabbed Jimmy, and stepped into the angry sea. I sheeted in and leaned back, not having to wait long before a gust hit the tiny sail. I pushed my front foot hard into the board and pulled the back under me with my back foot—and Jimmy planed out.

You know those cartoons where the character is going so fast that their lips pull back away from their teeth and jiggle like crazy?

You get the picture. I'm sure the wind and water were stinging my face, but damn, I felt nothing but pure joy. I made it to the island with lighting speed, approaching with a plan to jibe like the pros, almost teleporting to the other side, and heading back with a few minutes to spare. *Not.*

See, here is the thing about wind. It's unpredictable. Just as I was getting ready for my elegant maneuver, the wind calmed, the sail quieted, and my board sank.

No worries, I was at the island's rocky shore, standing in about three feet of water—and could feel the wind picking up again big time. I was about to lean way back and step on, grabbing onto the boom, when something slammed into my lower leg and almost knocked me into the sea. *Holy shit! What the fuck?* I jumped up on the rocks to figure out what the hell had just happened, when the searing pain registered. I looked down in horror at my torn and bleeding wetsuit.

Because of my pumping adrenaline, like a soldier in battle, I didn't feel the pain immediately. But I knew in an instant what had just happened. *Barracuda.* The Keys are full of them. I figured the sea was so churned up and murky with the big waves, he thought I was a fish.

Dread washed over me, as every cell in my body switched to survival mode. I was alone. I was bleeding big time. And I was terrified. Fear shook me to the core as I realized *no one was coming for me.*

I couldn't help but flash back for a moment to my life as a child—the abandonment that haunted me, and the sad realization that I could only really ever count on myself.

The storm was almost upon me—and the rest of the group on shore. I had to sail back.

The hardest thing I ever did in my entire life, no shit, was stepping back into the water. I remember reading that barracuda only bite once. So hoping with all get-out that my guy didn't have a bunch of buddies, I stepped in, grabbed Jimmy, lifted the sail, leaned back into the water, and said a prayer that I wouldn't faint from blood loss.

I took off almost violently, as the storm was nearly upon us.

I don't even remember how I made it back, as my friends told me I may have been in shock when they pulled me to shore. They had been beyond worried, ready to call the Coast Guard.

Evan was a volunteer firefighter and took charge. They carried me to his pickup, David jumped in the middle, and off we headed in the pelting rain to Fisher Community Hospital on Marathon Key. I drifted in and out of consciousness, and I may have had hypothermia, but Evan thought it was probably shock that caused me to shake uncontrollably.

The emergency team cut my new wet suit from ankle to hip, revealing fifteen perfectly-spaced puncture wounds, some as deep as two inches. I had a CT to make sure no teeth were left behind, and I mercifully had no bone damage. I needed several stitches for the large V-shaped lacerations and a tetanus shot, but otherwise I was happy as hell to be alive. The emergency room doc told me a barracuda had killed a man off Key West, and off the coast of North Carolina!

Everyone hooted and howled when we returned to camp, as this was before cell phones, and they were quite worried.

We all headed home the next day. Enough drama already. David drove the whole way home, back to Ohio. I was no help, painkillers and all.

From then on, I had a new respect—almost awe—for my Jimmy Lewis. He had saved my ass. I was so grateful that I decided to retire Jimmy; he earned his rest. We never sailed together again. I lovingly hung him high in my garage, where he stayed for twenty years. I eventually sold him at a garage sale at my future wife's urging, and I regret it to this day. *Sorry Jimmy.*

CHAPTER 30

Funny thing about being single. It's just great, and then one day it's not. I had married Loni twenty years ago and was divorced for nineteen. I started to miss having someone. David was away at college, and I was nearing forty.

A friend of mine kept mentioning a woman she knew who I should meet—a single mom with three teens. I said, "No way in hell," but she kept insisting, so I agreed.

We met for a glass of wine, and I asked her to marry me on our fourth date. Mom and Charlie loved her, as she would spoil them when they came to Ohio to visit every year. Mom had finally gotten sober at age sixty-five, and Charlie soon stopped drinking too. We went to Reading often to visit them as well, and one day we got a frantic phone call from Mom's trailer park manager.

Mom, Jeannie, and Charlie had been in a car accident. We quickly packed a few things, jumped in the car with our Australian Cattle dog, Katie, and drove through the night to Lehigh Hospital in Pennsylvania. We learned that Charlie was in intensive care with no hope of recovering. We begged the nurses to let us bring Katie in to see Charlie, as he loved Katie and would hang with her when they visited. Miraculously they said yes, and I carefully picked her up and placed her on the bed next to Charlie. We couldn't believe our eyes when he lifted his hand, placing it on Katie. Charlie died that night.

I spread his ashes at the famous Pagoda of Reading—a real, life-sized Chinese pagoda built on a small mountain just outside the city by an eccentric millionaire in 1908. Charlie loved to drive up there at night to see the lights of the city. Mom couldn't bear to go spread his ashes, so I drove up the mountain alone, climbed to the top floor of the Pagoda, opened the cardboard box, and watched his ashes disappear into the forest below.

I climbed down the massive steps, got into my car, and cried until I had nothing left. Charlie had come into my life when I was fourteen. He was the only grown-up who ever truly loved me. I guess my mother did too in her own way, but she had her own demons that had hardened her heart.

CHAPTER 31

After Charlie died, Mom's piercing green eyes lost their light, and she refused to drive again, having convinced herself that she had killed him. Thank God Walmart was just across the street from the trailer she shared with Jeannie. That worked for a while, until Mom lost her balance and fell in the middle of Bordic Road with a pushcart full of groceries. Jeannie started screaming and some nice guy in a pickup stopped and helped them home to their trailer. Mom wouldn't have told me about this incident, being too stubborn to admit she fell, but Jeannie did.

I knew they couldn't live alone. Mom was beginning to show signs of early dementia, often confused and forgetting words, which caused me great distress. Meanwhile, I was swamped at work, my wife had gone back to school full-time, and we had just bought a fixer-upper as an investment property.

But I had an idea.

My brother Willie, who had served seventeen of his twenty-five-year sentence, was out of prison and living in a row home in Reading while working a job driving a truck. I knew that he wanted nothing to do with our mother.

I had often thought about Willie and the terrible thing he had done. He had so much good in him too—I just knew he did—but no one had ever taught us right from wrong. I remember once as a child saying to my mother, "You don't love us, because you don't hit us." I guess I was trying to work it out as a child—why everyone else in our neighborhood would get a good spanking once in a while, while we never did. In fact, I witnessed many times my mother outright lying to the police to protect one of us from consequences. A part of me resented her for not helping us learn from them.

Even though I knew Willie would react negatively to any chance to see or help Mom, I decided to call him anyway. Instead, I asked him to help me find Tom.

He did. Willie called me back that very night.

"I found Tom living in a half-way house in Exeter, little bro'," he said. "I have a phone number where you can reach him."

I thanked Willie big-time, told him I loved him and said goodbye.

• • • • •

I was hesitant to call Tom. Regardless, I knew Tom loved Mom and Jeannie, so I called and offered him a deal. Tom could move in with Mom and Jeannie, take care of all their needs, and that would be his "job." He would cook, clean, take them to doctor appointments, etc., and in return he could use Mom's car and have access to the Social Security checks Mom and Jeannie got to pay bills and buy groceries. I didn't trust Tom, but I just didn't know what else to do.

I had to clear the arrangement with Tom's probation officer, and he agreed to it as long as Tom checked in with him once a week. I didn't even ask the officer what Tom had done this time to land on probation; I just couldn't bear any more bad news.

Things went well for a year or two. I think Tom was so grateful for a place to live and money to spend that he tried not to fuck up. In fact, Tom had learned early how to work the system—the social services system, that is. I swore if this guy used as much effort milking the system for free stuff as he did looking for honest work, he'd have become a CEO. Before you knew it, he was getting free massages intended for caregivers—and finagling a free home-care cleaning service and meals!

Mom and Jeannie loved having Tom there, as he was funny and played the guitar well. And Tom seemed to enjoy his newfound sense of importance. After a lifetime of incarcerations, couch surfing, and shelters, he had a room of his own in a spankin'-new double-wide, a checkbook, and a 1998 Honda Accord to drive around. Gas money too!

Then he fucked up. Of course he was going to fuck up. Major. I just didn't know about it until it was too late.

I had just left a managers' meeting at work when I got a call from a number I didn't recognize—a Pennsylvania area code, but it wasn't Mom's or Willie's phone number. I thought nothing of it and didn't listen to the message. A bit later, realizing I hadn't talked to Mom or Jeannie for a few days, I thought I better listen. Turns out it was the cleaning lady Tom had gotten from social services sounding alarmed. "Call me back right away," her message said.

She was so upset, I could hardly understand her. But I got the gist. Tom was in custody. Tom was going to prison. For three years. Wait for it… for domestic terrorism!

Now Tom had conspiracy theories like most nut jobs and always felt "the man" had stuck it to him, but I really thought he was relatively harmless. Turns out he was upset to learn that Mom's doctor had stopped accepting her supplemental Medicaid insurance. Why this set him off so badly, I have no idea, but he became extremely agitated and irrational, and decided to call his local senator to complain.According to court records, Tom called a senator's office in Reading, Pennsylvania. The office receptionist answered and testified that she spoke to Tom for about two minutes, during which he sounded very agitated, angry, and sarcastic. She then transferred the call to a colleague who handled social services issues. He took the call, and Tom complained that his mother was having trouble finding doctors who would accept her insurance. The social services specialist told Tom that the problem was an unfortunate but common one, and that he would be able to help.

Tom then became more agitated and angry during the course of the phone call. According to the specialist, "Mr. Olsen yelled that Clinton and NAFTA was 'fucking him in the ass without lube.' He also complained that his property taxes were also 'fucking him in the ass', and he was 'not happy with those kinds of situations'." The social services specialist also testified that Tom told him to "go back to my fat-ass swimming pool and my fat-ass job," and then directly after that, Tom yelled, "I'm going to shoot you in the fucking mouth with a shotgun, and everyone else in that office!'" Then Tom hung up.

The specialist testified that he interpreted Tom's words as a threat to his safety and the safety of his coworkers. He immediately ran to the receptionist's desk and had her press *69 to trace Tom's phone number. After hearing the phone number, they performed a Google search and determined the call had been made from a house in Exeter. They contacted the police, and an officer from the Reading Police Department arrived at the office within minutes.

After interviewing members of the office staff, the officer escorted the employees out of the office and to their vehicles, because they feared for their lives.

The officer then called the phone number in question and spoke with Tom. He testified that during his conversation, Tom ranted that "all politicians should be bombed and the country should start over again." Tom also stated that he wished the threat he made to the senator would come true. At that point, the officer informed Tom that he was going to be charged as a result of the threat. Later that evening, a judge signed a warrant for Tom's arrest.

Here is how it went down:

On May 10, 2011, following trial by jury, Tom was convicted of Count 1, Terrorist Threats, and Count 2, Harassment.

Tom was sentenced to twenty-three months in the Berk's County Prison, followed by a three year probation. Of course, upon hearing his sentence, Tom being Tom, he exploded into a tirade of foul language, screaming, among other things, "They fucking lied! They fucking lied! You fucking lied!" while pointing to the victims. Upon witnessing Tom's violent behavior, the Court cancelled any chance of a re-entry plan.Tom and his court-appointed attorney immediately filed an appeal. Like I said, my brother, who I once looked up to, knew the system. He was allowed to go home, pending appeal, and told no one what had happened. That's why we didn't find out for five months! The day of his appeal hearing, he had Mom and Jeannie get dressed early, and he dragged them to court with him. He had Mom use a walker for effect and instructed them to sit in the front row. I'm told Jeannie cried the whole time, thanks to Tom telling them if he went to prison, they would lose their home. Of course he was counting on the judge's sympathy when the judge saw his elderly mother and whimpering, mentally-disabled sister. It didn't work.

Appeal denied. I'm told they carried him out, kicking and screaming.

Tom had arranged for the cleaning lady to be at the courthouse just in case it didn't work out as planned, so Mom and Jeannie would have someone to take them home. That's how we finally found out what was going on. The cleaning lady had my number, hence the aforementioned phone call.

Now living 539 miles away, I had to figure something out. Quickly. I had one hope. Willie hated Mom. I mean he really, really hated her. I'm sure all those years behind bars, starting at fourteen, he had many nights to think about how life might have been different if Mom would have been different.

But I knew Willie loved me and Jeannie, so I called him. And damn if he didn't come through for me.

CHAPTER 32

Willie never got into trouble again after serving seventeen of his twenty-five-year sentence. He had been driving an eighteen-wheeler for a few years, even earning his One Million Miles belt buckle, a huge honor for a truck driver. He was living with his girlfriend, Donna, thirty years his junior, who had lost her kids due to her bipolar disorder. Somehow, they were perfect for each other.

When I hesitantly called him asking for help, explaining the situation as best I could, all he answered was, "Sure little brother, anything to help you."

I swear this guy turned into Dudley Do-Right after his release. One day the previous winter, he called to tell me he had shoveled all his neighbor's driveways after a heavy snowstorm. No charge! He and Donna even became volunteers with the Reading Fire and Rescue as "fire police." They would get called up at all hours to help direct traffic and keep rubberneckers away while the firefighters worked to contain the fire.

When I called, they drove right over to Mom's trailer, and I do believe that when Willie saw how feeble and confused she had become, he softened a bit. Donna had packed a few things, and she pretty much moved in—cooking and whatnot. Willie drove during the week, but he would sleep there on weekends.

This went on for maybe three months while my wife and I scrambled to switch all their medical and Social Security information to Michigan. We had recently moved there from Ohio, buying a cottage on the lake that my wife had noticed for sale when she was working nearby. It was only fifteen minutes from the Ohio border and a shorter drive to work for me than from our old house.

Sadly, we knew Mom needed to be in a nursing home, as her dementia was getting worse, and Donna had to call the police to come help her every time Mom fell. Miraculously, there was a spot open in a lovely facility about an hour south of us, on the scenic Maumee River. We were torn about getting Jeannie full-time help as well, but we knew she needed it, as she had recently been diagnosed with muscular dystrophy, and it was progressing rapidly.

The doctor Donna took her to in Reading said Jeannie had had it for years, but with no advocate looking out for her all those years in the Philadelphia Home for the Retarded, it was never addressed. I swore to myself I would never let that happen again to my sweet Jeannie. I would take care of her until her last breath.

I remembered how we had loved each other as kids. She was often my only friend. We had clung to each other desperately when no one else took care of us. And I recalled how devastated I was when I learned that Jeannie wouldn't be joining me and Tom at the orphanage, but instead was being sent far away to Philadelphia. With the help of social services, we were happy to find a highly-rated group home not far from us where Jeannie would have her own bedroom and weekly outings to a movie and the mall. My wife even took Jeannie to Ikea in her wheelchair, and they had a blast picking out furniture for Jeannie's new room.

Jeannie and Mom settled into their new respective homes, I sold the trailer, and life smoothed out again.

CHAPTER 33

I decided to find my sister, Rita. I told myself I just wanted to let her know all that had happened in the family.

I had heard bits and pieces through the years—that she was living in New Jersey, was married, and had a few children. We had spoken once or twice years ago, but it was often awkward—and well, I guess we both had just moved on.

I did find her—twice-divorced and living near Nashville, Tennessee; driving an eighteen-wheeler for Nissan; and living in a new double-wide. I invited her to visit, asking Rita "if you might like to make some kind of peace with Mom, before she dies," or "before Mom's dementia gets too bad." I feared Mom would die knowing nothing about the daughter she had tossed away, and that just didn't feel right.

I also thought of Rita and the pain she must carry.

She accepted my invitation and drove up to Michigan the following weekend. My God, she looked so much like our mother. Same green eyes. She must have held so much inside all these years, because as soon as we showed her to the guest room, she burst out crying. It broke our hearts to hear her pain.

"Rita, what's wrong, honey?" I asked. "Do you want to talk about it?"

She did. Years of hurt just came pouring out of her. It turns out my father's mother had shown up at the adoption proceedings and was embarrassed of what was going down—with her oldest son and his wife not wanting their baby girl and being willing to sign her over to a stranger.

"I'll take the baby," she had blurted out, without really thinking about it. So she did, but it was a baby she would resent bringing home the moment she walked in her door.

Rita told us she called our grandmother her "mother"—but was never shown an ounce of maternal love. She was never held or kissed, hugged or encouraged. Unbelievably, she was told that our father and our aunt and uncles were her siblings.

It gets worse. Rita said that when she was about eleven, our father took her into the woods by their house and sexually abused her. He didn't stop, so at sixteen, she dropped out of school, ran away, and got a job as an exotic dancer. She even went on to describe the club where she danced, explaining that "I spent my breaks in the office with the club's owners, drinking coffee and smoking their Camel cigarettes," because she was too young to be in a bar.

My wife and I were in tears as she shared her story. But it wasn't over.

She then told us that she had a baby at seventeen—"a beautiful, perfect baby girl," she said, her voice trembling—who she gave up the day the child was born. My wife asked about the father, and Rita said she was so ashamed, she couldn't begin to guess.

We all held each other and cried for a long time. Cried for all that we had lost. Or never had. Each other, our innocence, parents that loved us, a safe childhood, a normal family, Rita's baby girl.

All these years, I thought *at least my sister must have had a better life than we did,* but I was wrong.

At least we had found each other now, after all these years.

• • • • •

We drove down to the nursing home the next morning, and I could feel Rita's nervous heart. We decided to give them some time alone, so my wife and I waited in the hallway outside Mom's room. A while later, Rita came out, and I could feel something had happened; her face had softened so. Rita put her arms around me and sobbed. We stood there for a long time, no one saying a word.

Then she wiped her eyes and told us what had happened in that room.

When she entered, Rita had leaned over Mom's bed and said, "Hi Mom, it's Rita."

Mom had looked into her eyes and asked, "My Rita?"

Rita told her, "Yes, it's me, Mom."

And for the only time I could ever remember in my entire life, my mother said, "I'm sorry."

"The cure for the pain is the pain."

—Rumi

CHAPTER 34

My mother lived six more years—her mind deteriorating into the most heartbreaking of dementias, Lewy Body. She would have terrifying hallucinations and delusions, and would strike out physically—scratching and biting the staff. But thankfully, she slept most of the day.

She didn't know who I was anymore, and that was the most painful. Still, in the quiet of her room, gazing out at the late afternoon sky, I thought about my mother.

I don't know what makes a person matter to another person. I thought about my sister, Rita, who Mom gave away when she was three days old. I thought about Jeannie, alone in that terrible place for all those years. And I wondered why she took us back to the orphanage, dropping us off at the gate with no explanation, not even a goodbye, only weeks after picking us up.

My mother was like a wild animal most of her life. I realized I had never asked her what she was thinking, or if she was happy. I remembered my mother had never kissed me.

And as I drove home late that night, I wondered why I loved her.

• • • • •

We got the call early Saturday morning. Mom had finally died. My wife and I drove the hour down to the nursing home in silence.

I'm not sure there are words to describe my heart. The staff had moved her roommate and pulled the curtain around her bed. I slowly pulled it open.

She looked so small. Almost like she drew into herself. Even

THE PAGODA, READING, PENNSYLVANIA.

though I had just been there the day before, I'm not sure I would have recognized her. Her small hands were bluer than I remember, and felt cold in my hand. *Oh Momma.*

Nothing left to do, hospice would arrange the cremation. There would be no service, no casseroles, not a single flower. My mother didn't know a soul here, only the staff at the nursing home.

My wife and I would travel back to Reading the following summer to spread her ashes at the Pagoda, so she could be with Charlie.

CHAPTER 35

My father was a pedophile. There. I said it. I had my suspicions. That's why the police came up the mountain with that Mennonite man years ago, and my father disappeared soon after. It's why Lorraine, his third wife, threw him out just after her young granddaughter came to live with them. And the secret fell to my poor sister, Rita, who would confide in me years later what our father had done to her in the woods by my grandmother's house.

"There was a court case too," Rita said, "years ago."

A family accused him of molesting their young daughter. According to Rita, my grandmother gave him a perfect alibi, so it was her word against his, and well, they had to drop the case.

To say my father was the black sheep of his family would be, well, an immense understatement. He never finished high school, content to pick up odd jobs here and there. I'm told he drove a truck, and then, unbelievably, a school bus. I don't even want to think about that. After he left us and worked on the ocean liner, he returned to marry three more times.

He never tried to find us. I never received a card or a gift, not even a phone call the rest of my life. Probably the most painful part was when I learned years later from Willie that my father had returned to Reading to live just a few blocks from The Mission while Tom and I lived there. Who knows? Maybe Tom and I passed his house on our walk to school. *And I wondered how a father could be OK leaving such scars on his children.*

You already know that my father's family wanted nothing to do with us. I will never fully know why, but my grandmother hated my mother with such vile that she completely disengaged from us too, her own grandchildren. I knew nothing about my father's siblings: my aunt and uncles.

So you can imagine my wariness when decades later, my wife decided to find them for me.

CHAPTER 36

Thanks to the internet, my wife found my Aunt Louise living on Marco Island, Florida; my Uncle Jack in Arlington, Virginia; and my Uncle George living in San Antonio.

But what she found next is, well, I can only say you couldn't make this shit up if you tried.

My Aunt Louise, my father's only full sibling, joined the Air Force when she was nineteen. After serving four years, she left and went to college on the GI Bill, then put herself through law school. She was one of only eight women in her graduating class and went on to become a respected patent and trademark judge!

My Uncle George is a different story. Unbelievable really, but true. My wife found out that George was a criminal mastermind. Big time. I mean Bernie Madoff big time. This one will really blow your mind. This dude was smart.

Uncle George was president of Inverworld Securities Inc., a now closed investment firm in Texas. The United States Security and Exchange Commission alleged that since January 1, 1997, Inverworld managed approximately $433 million on behalf of at least 1,000 investors. Contrary to representations that client funds would be primarily in safe, secure investments, Inverworld instead invested in extremely risky and undisclosed offshore investments. They also grossly misrepresented the true value of client investments in monthly account statements and created a complex web of offshore entities to disguise the true nature of their activities!

Uncle George pleaded guilty to investment advisor fraud and conspiracy to launder money. On March 3, 2003, the court sentenced him to 84 months imprisonment and ordered criminal restitution of $139 million!

You and I both realize the irony here, no doubt. Tom and I were in the orphanage, and Jeannie in a mental institution, all while our uncle was a millionaire.

He served his time and was released from prison, and from what my wife could find, went on to live a quiet life in Texas.

My Uncle Jack was quite a bit younger than the others and worked for the National Geospatial-Intelligence Agency. I know. I had never heard of it either. It used to be called the Mapping Department. It's a combat support agency under the United States Department of Defense and a member of the United States Intelligence Community. Its primary mission is the collecting, analyzing, and distributing geospatial intelligence in support of our troops, especially in combat. Think about it. Someone has to learn the terrain and map out safe routes in war zones for our troops to move about on their missions.

And they have the coolest motto: "Know the Earth.....Show the Way.....Understand the World."

Uncle Jack was pretty high up in the Department, so he got to work on some way-cool stuff, including the moon landing and Desert Storm.

Wait, it gets better.

Uncle Jack was on the team that was vital in tracking down the whereabouts of Osama bin Laden! They helped pinpoint his compound in Abbottabad, Pakistan; study it meticulously; and plan the successful raid that killed him.

We couldn't believe the stuff my wife was finding out. My Uncle Jack represented the United States in more than forty countries, worked with the White House and Vice President Al Gore, and helped implement Geo-graphic Information Systems across government agencies. He gave forty-seven years of service to our government, but he didn't stop there.

According to my wife's research, after retirement, Uncle Jack continued his service to others. Looks like he became a favorite student mentor at his alma mater, George Mason University, where he recently set up an endowment fund at the university named the Jack Fahey Giving Back Scholarship.

To say I was stunned by my deadbeat father's siblings' incredible life stories wouldn't even get close to how I felt.

My wife decided to write a letter to each of them, even Uncle George, explaining that I was now married with children and grandchildren, and would love to talk with them about the side of my family I knew nothing about. She sent the letters off, fingers crossed.

My Aunt Louise never responded, nor did Uncle George. But a few weeks later, my Uncle Jack called.

And just like that, we were going to Thanksgiving dinner in Virginia.

• • • • •

I think my wife was more nervous than I was, fretting about what to wear, finally choosing a simple white shirt, gray skirt, and her mother's pearls. I couldn't decide, but settled on a sport coat, button-down, and Dockers. Silly, I know. Somehow thinking we had to show our worth.

We pulled up to a lovely home on a quiet street. I could feel my heart beating faster as we walked up the drive, my wife carrying a basket of our neighbor's organic soaps.

We opened the door to kids running, dogs barking, turkey roasting, and all the chaos that is Thanksgiving in a large family. A distinguished looking man greeted us with the biggest smile.

"Rob! Welcome! I'm your Uncle Jack!" He kindly took our coats and told us to make ourselves at home. We braved our way into the crowded kitchen and hoped for the best.

Uncle Jack returned with two glasses of wine and started introducing us around. He said Uncle George wasn't coming, his health in decline, probably never quite recovering from his long incarceration, but I met cousins I didn't know—wonderful, warm and interesting people. I learned that my cousin, Romain, became an actor on Broadway! I found out I'm Jewish, and that my fourth great-grandfather was named Zadoc Isaacs, and was the head undertaker for the largest synagogue in London! My cousin, Michelle, showed me an old photo she had found of his gravestone, complete with all of his twelve children listed by name.

I could hardly take it all in.

I felt a bit hesitant to meet Aunt Louise, who had driven up with her husband, Don, from Florida—given that she never responded to my wife's letter. Turns out my wife ran into her first, on her way back from the bathroom. I was a little worried about this happening.

My wife sometimes gets angry about no one coming to rescue me from The Mission. "Who are these people?" she would ask.

"What kind of person lets this happen to children in their own family?" I mean she can't wrap her head around it. She came from a family the polar opposite of mine. She once told me that as a child, she knew in her heart that if she were ever lost or sick or kidnapped or anything, her father would find her and take her home. He would never, never, ever stop looking—never give up until he found her. She felt his fierce and complete love for his children, who he would move mountains for.

She found a tiny, fragile-looking older lady in the hall. "Are you Louise? Aunt Louise?"

My wife said she just couldn't help herself. "It's a shame you never knew your nephew, Rob. He is a remarkable man. A wonderful man. Our children adore him. Do you know he put himself through Ohio State? And is highly respected in the large company he works for? Quite remarkable for a boy who grew up in an orphanage, don't you think?"

Holy Moly.

Aunt Louise said no, she didn't know, and yes, it is quite remarkable, and that she better sit down. She made a beeline for Uncle Jack, and I know she filled him in on my wife's not-so-warm introduction.

Then my aunt and uncle asked to speak with me. We found a quiet corner, and Aunt Louise rested her hand on my arm.

What they told me was almost exactly what played out in my head on our drive to Virginia. What I longed to hear. That they didn't know. That they would have helped had they known. That they were sorry. So very sorry. And how glad they were that we had come, and could we stay in touch.

We ended up having a wonderful, heartwarming visit. Hugs all around, as we said our goodbyes, with promises to stay in touch.

The last thing my Aunt Louise said to me that day as we were leaving caught me off guard. "He was a bad man. Your father. A bad, bad man."

CHAPTER 37

I read something once that film director and cinematographer Eric Saarinen said about forgiveness.

His father, Eero Saarinen, was a modernist architect, a bit of a rock star really, known for his neo-futuristic style and wildly popular tulip chair.

Eric talks about his almost violent uprooting from his beloved home in Bloomfield Hills, Michigan, a 300-acre sprawling art institute and academy with rolling hills, woods, and streams—a child's paradise. His father had fallen in love with an art critic from the *New York Times* who came to interview him one day, and soon he and his mother were cast out like yesterday's news.

He hated his father viciously for many years, and then, slowly, something began to change. He wrote, "Suddenly, I was forgiving my father. But it's a process. You can forgive, little by little. It doesn't happen all at once."

I know that is true. I don't think much about my father anymore, but when I do, the hurt has lost a lot of its sting.

CHAPTER 38

The wonderful writer Joanne Fedler once wrote, "In owning our stories, we magically, paradoxically, are able to let them go. That's the deal the muse has struck with life. Own it. Really own it. And it will let you leave without the pain."

I've been married twenty-eight years now. We live in a small cottage on Lake Erie, and for the most part, I wake up happy and grateful. I love to watch the storms roll in from a good nor'easter, enjoy sailing my little Hobie on the perfect wind, and feeling a thrill as I watch the eagles soar above the lake in all their majesty.

Willie rides his Harley out every year for a visit, and Rita drives up from Nashville when she can. I haven't heard from Tom in years, and that's just fine with me.

All in all, I've had a good life.

Heck, I've seen the pyramids. Hiked to the top of Mount Sinai. Snowboarded Andorra. Climbed the Eiffel Tower. Raced the Ice Man Cometh. Walked the Camino. Ate squid in its own ink. Adore my grandchildren, love my wife.

• • • • •

I traveled back to Reading a few years ago to visit the orphanage. The old building still stands, but looks different, now painted white. It is no longer a Children's Home, but a social services and juvenile drug rehab center. I hoped to find records of my years there, and maybe even the name of my Sunday dinner family so I could thank them. I was heartsick to discover that a fire had destroyed all the records in 1972.

The current director was kind enough to meet me there on a warm Saturday afternoon for a tour of the building. The large living room I remembered was now remodeled into several offices. Same with our large dining room. I hardly recognized it. My disappointment grew when we toured the second floor. It had also been cut up into small offices. But when we climbed the stairs to the third floor, I felt my heart quicken.

There it was. My old sleeping dormitory. The same high gable windows I used to gaze out of into the night sky. The three small built in drawers, every few feet or so, that sat between our beds, holding the clothing and secrets of each child. The same old wood floor that creaked the way I remembered.

I had to sit down for a moment. It was almost too much. I walked past the jumble of storage boxes and file cabinets, over to where my bed had stood. I remembered my young self, confused and frightened, curling up under my thin blanket, praying that it was all a dream. But it wasn't. I had lived here.

• • • • •

By the time my father died at ninety, diabetes had taken most of one leg and the toes of the other one. He died alone in a state-run nursing home. I had not seen or heard from him in forty years.

Willie called early one morning with the news. "The old man died."

"OK, thanks," I heard myself say. "I'll call you back." I remember hanging up the phone and laying my head back down. Gazing out at the still-dark morn, I saw the moon was quite full, casting a beautiful glow on the lake. I pulled my wife's warm body closer to mine.

I don't know why, but I asked Willie for just a small amount of his ashes. My wife and I headed to Pennsylvania and picked them up, tucked into a small blue envelope, then drove to the mountain.

The twin churches came into sight, as we made our way up the winding dirt road. The house was still there too, although it looked a bit different, the bushes grown tall. There was a pickup in the yard, so we drove around to one of the old churches. It looked a bit run-down, probably closed for years. We got out and walked past the small, overgrown cemetery we used to play in as kids. The sky was so blue.

This is where he left us. This is where I will leave him.

I took my wife's hand in mine—as his ashes lifted in the light wind, circled, and danced down the mountain.

Both of us, free.

A WORD FROM C.L. OLSEN

Sincere thanks to my able research assistant, journalist Teddy Angert, and to my supportive and talented editor, Jocelyn Carbonara—and most importantly to my amazing husband Rob, who trusted me enough to share his story.

clolsenwrites@gmail.com

Made in USA - Kendallville, IN
18328_9798521787425
05.13.2023 1307